T0299431

CATALOGUS LIBRORUM MANUSCRIPTORUM
BIBLIOTHECAE WIGORNIENSIS

CATALOGUS
LIBRORUM MANUSCRIPTORUM
BIBLIOTHECAE WIGORNIENSIS

MADE IN 1622–1623

by

PATRICK YOUNG

LIBRARIAN TO KING JAMES I

Edited with an Introduction by

IVOR ATKINS

LIBRARIAN OF WORCESTER CATHEDRAL

and

NEIL R. KER

LECTURER IN PALAEOGRAPHY IN THE
UNIVERSITY OF OXFORD

CAMBRIDGE
AT THE UNIVERSITY PRESS

1944

CAMBRIDGE
UNIVERSITY PRESS

University Printing House, Cambridge CB2 8BS, United Kingdom

Cambridge University Press is part of the University of Cambridge.

It furthers the University's mission by disseminating knowledge in the pursuit of education, learning and research at the highest international levels of excellence.

www.cambridge.org
Information on this title: www.cambridge.org/9781107536869

© Cambridge University Press 1944

This publication is in copyright. Subject to statutory exception and to the provisions of relevant collective licensing agreements, no reproduction of any part may take place without the written permission of Cambridge University Press.

First published 1944
First paperback edition 2015

A catalogue record for this publication is available from the British Library

ISBN 978-1-107-53686-9 Paperback

CONTENTS

CONTENTS

INTRODUCTION

IT is unfortunate that the library of Worcester Cathedral, though ranking so high among the great medieval monastic libraries of England, possesses no ancient catalogues such as we find at Durham, Canterbury, and other great Churches. Indeed, apart from the brief list of Anglo-Saxon books in an eleventh-century Worcester manuscript now at Corpus Christi College, Cambridge—almost certainly a list of books which then belonged to Worcester monastery—no further ancient record of the contents of the library has survived.[1] In fact until the unexpected appearance of the catalogue now lying before us the earliest examples which Worcester possessed were two catalogues drawn up after the Restoration.

The first of these is still in manuscript and is to be found in Bodleian MS. Tanner 268, where it is one of a collection of catalogues which appear to have been compiled in the second half of the seventeenth century. The second, a recension of the first, was printed in Bernard's *Catalogi MSS. Angliæ et Hiberniæ* (Oxford, 1697).

The discovery, therefore, in 1941 of a full catalogue which antedated the earliest known Worcester catalogues by some forty or fifty years was hailed as a major event in the history of the library. A carefully detailed enumeration of the manuscripts at Worcester in the early years of the seventeenth century was likely to be valuable. Evidently such a catalogue could afford only partial help in reconstructing the picture of the library as it was in medieval times, since the extent of its losses after the Reformation would remain an unknown quantity. But there was the possibility that, having been drawn up before the upheavals of the Civil War, the catalogue might open up a considerably widened vista of the library's ancient past. This hope has been abundantly justified.

The catalogue which lies before us is one of five which formed part of a large collection of Selden and Hale papers belonging to Mr James Fairhurst of Oldham. These catalogues, each of which is marked B. 29, describe the manuscripts in the Cathedral libraries of Lichfield, St Paul's, Salisbury, Worcester and Winchester. All of them belonged to Selden, and are mentioned as follows on f. 13ᵛ of the second part of a list of Selden's books and manuscripts, now also in the possession of Mr Fairhurst:

29. Catalogue (in loose sheetes) MS. 4to of the MSS. in several Cathedralls etcetera in England (videlicet)

1	In Lichfeild library pag. 1	2	In Pauls London pag. 5
3	In Salisburie pag. 13	4	Worcester pag. 23

[1] It is very improbable that the book-list in Bodleian MS. Tanner 3 relates to Worcester. For the list see H. M. Bannister in *English Historical Review*, XXXII (1917), 388.

    5   Græcorum penes Patricium Junium pag. 40
    6   MSorum in Bibliotheca Winton pag. 41.

Item 5 in this list has not been found. Items 1–4 and 6 are in the
hand of Patrick Young, librarian successively to Prince Henry, James I
and Charles I, prebendary of St Paul's in 1621, and perhaps the chief
Greek scholar of his time. Mr Fairhurst took the view that the catalogues
ought to belong to the Cathedrals concerned and gave the Chapter
of Worcester the opportunity of acquiring the Worcester catalogue in
1941. The other four catalogues also are now in the respective Cathedral
libraries.

    The manuscript of the catalogue, now Worcester Cathedral Add. MS.
190, consists of sixteen folio pages, numbered 23–38. Pages 23–35 contain
the list of the 343 Cathedral manuscripts,[1] page 36 is taken up with
notes of manuscripts which belonged to Thomas Allen,[2] and to Gilbert
Talbot, ninth earl of Shrewsbury (d. 1630), at Grafton near Broms-
grove,[3] page 37 is blank, and the last page gives some account of the
contents of the Worcester cartulary, Cotton Tiberius A. xiii.

    The compilation of the catalogue must have occupied Young for a
considerable time, but how long it is impossible to say, for there is no
reference to his visit in the Chapter records, which for this period are
unusually bare. The reasons for his visit are disclosed in an entry in the
Calendar of State Papers (Domestic) for 1622, which shows that in July of
that year the King issued a 'Warrant for payment of £100, and more
if needful, to Patrick Young, Keeper of the King's libraries, appointed
to make search in all cathedrals for old manuscripts and ancient
records, and to bring an inventory of them to His Majesty'. Probably,
therefore, Young visited Worcester. While there he occupied himself
in compiling a catalogue of the Cathedral manuscripts and in making
an Epitome of the important First Register. The Epitome was published
by Hearne in 1723—just a hundred years later.[4] The catalogue has
had to wait until now. His task completed, Young no doubt discussed
with friends like Bishop John Williams, then dean of Westminster
and Lord Keeper, the various discoveries he had made in the Cathedral libraries. For, as we shall see later,[5] the dean and Chapter on

---

[1] The manuscripts are divided into three classes, Folio, Quarto and Octavo, and
the variations from the normal size are recorded, e.g. 'large' (or 'mag') and 'litle'.
The total number of folios is 215 (194 'fol.', 20 'fol. litle', and 1 'fol. large'), of
quartos 90 (87, and 3 'litle'), and of octavos 37 (34, with 2 'mag' and 1 'litle').
These together with one manuscript whose size Young forgot to specify (no. 321)
make up a grand total of 343.

[2] Thomas Allen (1542–1632), mathematician and collector of manuscripts, most
of which are now in the Digby collection in the Bodleian.

[3] Grafton House was almost completely destroyed by fire in 1710.

[4] 'Chartularii Wigorniensis Epitome per Patricium Junium', pp. 513–51 of T.
Hearne, *Hemingi chartularium ecclesiæ Wigorniensis* (1723). Hearne's text is from Young's
autograph in Cotton Vitellius C. ix. The First Register is now A. iv.

[5] *Vide infra* (p. 3), Chapter Minute of 3 February 1624/5.

25 November 1623 were deliberating upon letters directed to them from James I asking, as they record, 'for all such dubble maniscripts as we have dubble in our liberary'. The manuscripts were to be sent to the Lord Keeper towards the furnishing of the library which he was then building at Westminster Abbey.

The request is strangely phrased, but, as no copy of the King's letter was entered in the Chapter Minutes, we do not know that it has been reproduced in the language of the original. It is clear, however, that what was meant was that where there were two copies of a work in the library one was to be given to Bishop Williams for his new library. It is strange that there is no direct mention of the King's letter in the Minutes of the meeting of 25 November, but only an Order making 'A graunt to my Lord Keeper of such Manuscripts as we have double in our librarie towards the furnishing of his library at Westminster'.[1]

More than a year passed before any further action was taken. The delay may have been occasioned by the fact that the librarian, Dr John Archbold, prebendary of the fourth stall, died in December 1623. The appointment of his successor who, as Canon J. M. Wilson conjectures,[2] was probably the learned Henry Bright, headmaster of the Cathedral school and one of the prebendaries, could not have been made until the following year, and one can readily understand that the new librarian would need time to familiarize himself with the contents of the library before being able to make sure of the right choice of the manuscripts for Westminster.[3]

It was not until 3 February 1624/5 that the matter was again deliberated by the Chapter in the absence of the dean, who appears to have been in London. By this time the books intended for Westminster had been chosen and the members then present, Richard Potter, subdean, and prebendaries William Barkesdale and Henry Bright, took action as recorded in the following Minute:

[*Acta Capituli*, Worcester Cathedral Muniments, A. lxxv, f. 84ᵛ]

3 FEBRUARY 1624(/5). Whereas letters from his Majesty directed unto us under the Great Seale of England for all such dubble maniscripts as we have dubble in our liberary towards the furnishing of a liberarie in the Church of Westminster newly erected or augmented by the nowe Lord Keper   Whereuppon wee consented as by our Chapter act bearing date the xxvth day of Novemb: 1623 doth appeare   Nowe wee whose names are subscribed by virtue

---

[1] A. lxxv, f. 81ᵛ. The Minutes were signed by Joseph Hall, dean, and by John Charlet, John Archbold, Henry Bright and Eustacius Moore, prebendaries.

[2] J. M. Wilson, 'The Library of Printed Books in Worcester Cathedral', in *The Library*, 3rd Series, II (1911), p. 10. Canon J. M. Wilson was Cathedral librarian from 1907 to 1923.

[3] Or it may have been that there was no great urgency in the matter, for the work of rebuilding which Bishop Williams was carrying out at Westminster was done between the years 1623 and 1626 (Lawrence E. Tanner, *The Library and Muniment Room* (Westminster Papers, no. 1, 1933), p. 6).

of the said letters and consent of the Dean and Chapter and as by a letter from Mr. Deane unto us of the Chapter bearing date the xxɪɪnd day of January 1624[/5] have sent upp the sd maniscripts unto Mr. Deane to London for the better conveying thereof, and to the said purpose appointed vizt.

	[Young No.	Worcester]
Augustinus de Civitate Dei[1]	16 or 17	—
Idem de verbis Domini	19	F. 32
Anselmi varia	33	F. 41
Gregorii Pastorale[2]	37 or 38	—
Prophetæ 12 cum glossa	60	Q. 8
Psalterium cum glossa	79	F. 47
Pauli epistolæ cum glossa	81	F. 49
Historia Scholastica	91 or 93	F. 37
Vocabularium Bibliorum Huberti monachi cui titulus Prometheus	103	F. 61
Sermones Jacobi de Losanna de sanctis	110	Q. 19
Magister Sententiarum	One of 128–133	F. 2, etc.
Determinationes quotlibetorum Henrici de Gandavo	158	F. 79
Digestum novum	171 or 172	F. 136
Innocentius in decretales	176 or 177	F. 170
Decretales cum glossa	188 or 189	F. 59
Concordantia discordantium canonum	204 or 205	F. 120
Breviarium extravagantium Bernardi Papiensis	213	F. 122
Legenda sanctorum Jacobi Januensis	248	F. 45
Brito Vocabularius	282	F. 13
Prisciani grammatica[2]	291 or 292	—

    Richardus Potter, *subdecanus.*
    W. Barkesdale, *Recever.*[3]
    Henry Bright.

To the list given here we have added in two columns the number of each manuscript in Young's catalogue and the number of the existing Worcester volume of which it was a duplicate. As will be seen, every manuscript which Westminster should have had can be identified in Young's catalogue. Indeed it is likely that the catalogue was used when the selection was made, for the twenty manuscripts are listed in the very order in which Young described them. What happened to the books after they left Worcester is not known. They were sent direct to the Dean of Worcester (Joseph Hall, Dean 1616–27) in London 'for the better conveying thereof'. What is meant by these words is not clear, but it may be that the Chapter had in mind that their dean would make formal presentation of the manuscripts to the Lord Keeper at Westminster. From the time of their leaving Worcester the books

---

[1] The existing copy of this work (F. 171) is an eighteenth-century addition to the library.
[2] There is no longer a copy of this work in the library.
[3] *i.e.* Receiver-General, an office held by one of the senior prebendaries.

completely disappeared. There is no record of their having been received at Westminster, nor are they traceable in the three seventeenth-century Westminster catalogues.[1] Dr Montague James regarded it as 'extremely doubtful whether they ever arrived at the library'.[2] Yet it seems certain that they left Worcester.

We can now indicate the losses which Worcester library has suffered since 1622-3. In addition to the twenty sent to Westminster seventy-one manuscripts listed by Young are no longer in the library. Only five of these are to be found in the later seventeenth-century catalogues.[3] The remainder must be presumed to have disappeared between 1622-3 and 1697.

MANUSCRIPTS LISTED BY PATRICK YOUNG IN 1622-3, which have been alienated from Worcester[4]

Manuscripts marked with an asterisk have already been assigned conjecturally to Worcester. Their presence in Young's catalogue confirms their Worcester provenance. Those marked + are now for the first time shown to be Worcester books.

Young No.		Present location, where known
3	Hieronymus in 12 prophetas	? B.M., Royal 4 C. ii, s. xii*
5	Hieronymus in psalmos	B.M., Royal 4 A. xiv, s. x+
6	Hieronymus in epistolas canonicas	B.M., Royal 2 D. xxvi, s. xiii *in.*
12	Exodus cum glossa	—
13	Ruth cum glossa	—
16 or 17	Augustinus de civitate Dei	—
18	Augustinus de verbis Domini	? B.M., Royal 5 C. ii, s. xiii+
20	Augustinus, Confessiones, vetus	—
21	Augustinus de libero arbitrio, etc.	—
22	Augustinus de mendacio, etc.	B.M., Royal 5 A. xiii, s. xii
23	Augustinus contra 5 hæreses, etc.	—
24	Augustinus in apocalypsin	Bodleian, Hatton 30, s. x
25	Augustinus, Retractationes, etc.	B.M., Royal 5 A. xiv, s. xii+
26	Registrum Gregorii	B.M., Royal 6 C. vii, s. xii*
28	Epistolæ Hieronymi	? B.M., Royal 6 D. iii, s. xii+
35	Quæstiones Isidori, etc.	B.M., Royal 5 E. v, s. xii+
36	Vita Gregorii	B.M., Royal 6 A. vii, s. xi *in.**
37 or 38	Pastorale Gregorii	? Glasgow, Hunterian V. 5. 1, s. x and xii*
39	Pastorale Gregorii, etc.	B.M., Royal 5 E. xii, s. xiii+
41	Fulgentius de fide Donato, etc.	B.M., Royal 5 B. iii, s. xii+

[1] Nor did they find their way to the library at St John's, Cambridge, which Bishop Williams was then building and furnishing.

[2] J. A. Robinson and M. R. James, *The Manuscripts of Westminster Abbey*, 1909, p. 103. In 1695 (for the date see L. E. Tanner, *op. cit.* p. 7) there was a fire in the library, and of the 230 manuscripts only one, the famous Islip Roll, is now in existence.

[3] Y. 183, 252 and 275 in Bodleian MS. Tanner 268; Y. 167 and 293 in Hopkins's 1697 catalogue.

[4] This list does not include those entries in Young's catalogue which have been tentatively identified with entries in the later Worcester catalogues (see Appendix I).

Young No.		*Present location, where known*
53	Lanfrancus de corpore Domini, etc.	B.M., Royal 5 F. xii, s. xii[+]
54	Admonitiones simplices parrochiis necessariæ, charactere Saxonico	—
55	Biblia latina	Bodleian, Auct. D. inf. 2.4, s. xiii
56	Comment. in psalmos anonymi	—
59	Jeremias et Daniel glosati	B.M., Royal 3 A. viii, s. xiii
61	Expositio in 12 prophetas et Job	B.M., Royal 2 E. xi, s. xiii *ex.*
67	Epistolæ Pauli glosatæ	B.M., Royal 2 F. i, s. xiii *in.*
70	Expositio Bedæ in Marcum, etc.	B.M., Royal 4 B. xiii, s. xii *ex.*[+]
73	Epistolæ Ambrosii, etc.	? B.M., Royal 6 A. xvi, s. xii[+]
74	Postills in English	—
98	Expositiones ex diversis patribus in Evangeliis et Epistolis	Bodleian, Barlow 4, s. xi *in.*[+]
102	Summa J. de Rupella, etc.	—
119	Sermones varii anonymi	—
167	Institutiones cum glossa	B.M., Harley 4967[+]
183	Leges et decreta Gratiani	—
192	Isidorus de originibus	—
199	Summa Godfredi super titulis decretalium	Worcester, F. 17 (*now missing*)
216	Regula S. Benedicti	Bodleian, Hatton 48, s. viii[+]
217	Smaragdi abbatis expositio in regulam S. Benedicti	Bodleian, Hatton 40, s. xii
218	Vita S. Modwennæ, etc.	B.M., Royal 15 B. iv, s. xii/xiii[+]
221	Excerpta ex synodis, etc.	Bodleian, Hatton 42, s. ix[+]
222	Collationes Joh. heremitæ	Bodleian, Hatton 23, s. xi*
223	De officio missæ, charactere Saxonico	Bodleian, Hatton 93, s. viii/ix*
235	Sermones de virginibus	—
240	Regimen animarum	Bodleian, Hatton 11, s. xv *in.*[+]
252	Liber precum in festis Sanctorum	—
253	Aldelmus de virginitate, charactere Saxonico	B.M., Royal 5 F. iii, s. ix/x[+]
257	Concilium Ottoboni, etc.	—
275	Gerardinus de modo medendi, etc.	—
286	Vita Barlaam et Josaphat, etc.	B.M., Harley 5394[+]
291 or 292	Grammatica Prisciani	B.M., Royal 15 B. xiv, s. xii *ex.*
293	De virtute lapidum, etc.	—
296	Liber grammaticalis (A. Nequam)	—
297	Missale cum notis musicis	—
298	Missale aliud cum notis musicis	—
301	Homilia anon.	—
305	Commentum Duncaht	B.M., Royal 15 A. xxxiii, s. x *in.**
309	Precationes quædam, charactere Saxonico	? B.M., Royal 2 A. xx, s. viii[+]
316	Fragmentum passionum quorumdam Sanctorum	—

Young No.		Present location, where known
317	Sermones Saxonici	Bodleian, Hatton 115, s. xi *ex.*
318	Sermones Saxonici	Bodleian, Hatton 113, s. xi
319	Sermones Saxonici	Bodleian, Hatton 114, s. xi
320	Sermones Saxonici	Bodleian, Hatton 116, s. xii
321	Constitutiones lingua Saxonica	Bodleian, Junius 121, s. xi
322	Dialogi Gregorii, etc., Saxonicè	Bodleian, Hatton 76, s. xi
324	Compilatio decretorum Ivonis, etc.	Bodleian, Hatton 6, s. xiii *in.*[+]
330	Smaragdus de diversis virtutibus	B.M., Royal 8 D. xiii, s. xii *in.*
333	Cypriani testimoniale	B.M., Royal 5 E. xiii, s. ix *ex.*[+]
337	Sermones duo lingua Saxonica, etc.	—
339	Retractationes Augustini, etc.	—
342	Compendium Veteris Testamenti	? Eton College, 96, s. xiii *med.*[+]
343	A missal in English	—

Besides these seventy-two entries in Young's catalogue which cannot be identified at all with extant manuscripts at Worcester there are some entries which can only be identified doubtfully, since many of Young's titles are very brief, and those applied to the legal books and the service-books are sometimes, we may suspect, inexact.[1] It has seemed well, however, to dispense with a query whenever a description in Young fits an extant Worcester manuscript exactly and to draw attention only to the considerable element of doubt in the identification of the following numbers:

Young
57	Psalterium et pars missalis	? F. 160 Antiphonarium, etc.
175	Decretalium liber sextus unde multa excisa	? F. 97 Apparatus sexti libri decretalium per G. de Baysio
209	Apparatus domini Guidonis supra extravagantes Joh. papæ	? F. 168 J. Andree apparatus in Clementinas, Extravagantes Joh. xxii, etc.
314	Homiliæ quædam laceræ	? Q. 100 Sermones (damaged by damp)

Young's catalogue does not include Hatton 20, the ninth-century Anglo-Saxon version of the 'Regula Pastoralis' of St Gregory the Great presented to the Church of Worcester by King Alfred, but with this exception all the books constituting the famous Worcester group of Anglo-Saxon manuscripts in the Hatton collection are to be found in the catalogue, nos. 317–22. The catalogue shows, too, the presence in the library at that time of the eighth-century copy of the Benedictine

[1] Four manuscripts now at Worcester and almost certainly there in 1622 cannot be identified with any of Young's descriptions. One of them, Q. 32, a thin collection of fragments of a glossed Isaiah and other texts, may have been passed over by Young owing to its evident lack of interest. The second and third are law books: F. 29, the commentaries of Azo on the Code, labelled in the late Middle Ages 'Commenta Justiniani', and F. 58, containing a 'Breviarium de jure canonico' and 'Goffredus super titulis decretalium'. The fourth, F. 173, is a fragment of an eleventh-century Sacramentary written for the Old Minster at Winchester.

Rule (Young no. 216, now Hatton 48), of which it is not too much to say that, as the oldest copy of the Rule extant, it is an object of veneration to every member of the Benedictine Order throughout the world.[1] It has hitherto been ascribed to Canterbury, where indeed it may have been written.[2]

It would be interesting, if it were possible, to trace the process by which from about the middle of the sixteenth century to the last quarter of the seventeenth the Cathedral was gradually despoiled of some of its greatest literary treasures. But we have as yet too little information to enable such a task to be undertaken with any prospect of success. It must suffice to touch upon the history of the spoliation in the briefest way.

It seems unlikely that the library suffered much before the Reformation. There would be, no doubt, the usual minor losses which were inevitable in a library not subject to the stringent regulations which are customary in great libraries to-day.

The earliest known loss is a copy of the Sentences, c. 1300, now Peterhouse, Cambridge, MS. 71, which is entered in the catalogue of the College Library compiled in 1418. It bears the inscription 'Memoriale fratris Roberti de Dikklesdon Monachi Wygornensis ecclesie'.[3]

Another book which may have strayed at an early date is now Bodley 223 (*Summary Catalogue* 2106), which came to the Bodleian from the dean and canons of Windsor in 1612. Its flyleaves contain Worcester documents and the script of the main text, Gregory on Ezekiel, suggests that the book was written at Worcester in the time of St Wulstan.

The period of the real losses seems to have begun towards the middle of the sixteenth century. It is convenient to date it from the visit paid by John Leland, the King's antiquary, between 1534 and 1543.[4] The ten Worcester books which found their way into the library of Henry VIII may well have been selected by him.[5] They are handsome folios of theology and law of the twelfth, thirteenth and fourteenth centuries.

[1] Dr H. H. E. Craster wrote of this manuscript: 'It is the most ancient copy of a document of prime importance in the history of religion and learning' (in E. A. Lowe, *Regula S. Benedicti*, Oxford, 1929, p. 5).

[2] See N. R. Ker, 'The Provenance of the Oldest Manuscript of the Rule of St Benedict' (*Bodleian Library Record*, vol. II, no. 17, 1941, p. 28).

[3] Robert of Diclesdon was made a penitentiary by Bishop Walter Reynolds in 1308 and was eighth in seniority amongst the monks in 1317. Six examples of the use of 'Memoriale' in book-inscriptions are given by M. R. James, *Descriptive Catalogue of the Manuscripts in the Library of Corpus Christi College, Cambridge*, I, 405. The word sometimes appears to mean 'keepsake', but, as Dr R. W. Hunt has pointed out to us, it certainly means 'pledge' in some instances.

[4] In 1533 Leland received a commission empowering him to make a search after England's antiquities and to peruse the libraries of all cathedrals, colleges, etc. His commission seems to have covered much the same ground as that of Patrick Young.

[5] They are now B.M. Royal 2 C. vii, 2 E. vi, 4 B. iv, 4 D. xii, 5 C. vi, 9 B. v, 9 B. xii, 11 B. ii, Corpus Christi College, Cambridge, 217, Oxford, Bodleian, Bodl. 862 (*S.C.* 2730). The two last are in the velvet bindings, with metal corner pieces, bosses and clasps, which clothe a number of the King's books outside the present Royal collection.

A peculiarity about them is that they all contain the inscription 'Liber monasterii Wygornie', instead of the 'Liber ecclesie cathedralis (beate Marie) Wygorn'', or 'Liber sancte Marie Wygorn'', found usually in Worcester books which bear a medieval inscription.[1] The form 'Liber monasterii Wygornie' is parallel to the 'Liber monasterii Eveshamie' found in two other manuscripts which were formerly in the King's library.[2] It seems likely that this form of inscription is a memorandum inserted at the time a manuscript was chosen for the King, in order to identify the library from which it was drawn, and that it is in fact of the same non-monastic kind as the inscriptions found in books from Cirencester, Bardney and Pershore which came into the King's hands.[3]

About twenty years later the real dismemberment of the library began. Serious inroads were made upon its manuscripts by Archbishop Parker, who succeeded in gaining possession of at least eleven important codices, four of them entirely in Anglo-Saxon. How he acquired them, or upon what terms, is not known. At his death all these Worcester manuscripts—save one which he had given to Cambridge University Library in 1574—passed by his bequest to Corpus Christi College, Cambridge. What Parker's object was in assembling them we know from Strype. 'Our archbishop', he says, '...was desirous to inquire everywhere for Saxon and British antiquities for the better knowledge of the history of the ancient state of this Church and nation'.[4] There is piety of purpose in this. We must let it go at that. And whether Parker's action was just or unjust, we shall do well to remember that its effect has been to assure the safety of these books for the generations to come.

The archbishop seems to have approached the Cathedral libraries through his diocesans. Thus he writes to John Scory, bishop of Hereford, in January 1565/6:

I geve you thankes for that you dydd not forgett to cause Hereford librarie to be serched for Saxon bookes.

[1] Three other books contain the inscription 'Liber monasterii Wygornie':
(a) Royal 10 B. x, which belonged to Lord Lumley (1534?–1609) and may have been formerly in the King's library.
(b) Worcester Cath. F. 79, which does not appear to have left Worcester, but was perhaps selected for the King and afterwards discarded. It has the inscription in the same sixteenth-century hand as that in Bodl. 862. The book contains the 'Quodlibeta' of Henricus de Gandavo, another copy of which, now Royal 11 C. x, was in the old Royal library.
(c) B.M., Harley 1659, W. Peraldus, De vitiis et virtutibus, which belonged to William Cecil, Lord Burleigh (1520–1598), and was in the sale of his manuscripts in 1687.
Corpus Christi College, Cambridge, MS. 24 may also have this form of inscription, but only 'Liber monasterii' is legible.
[2] Bodleian MS. Auct. D. 1. 15 (S.C. 2239) and Queen's College, Oxford, MS. 302.
[3] See N. R. Ker, Medieval Libraries of Great Britain (Royal Hist. Soc. 1941), p. xvi.
[4] Strype, Life of Matthew Parker (Clarendon Press, 1821), I, 417. See also Parker's own statement in the Preface to A Testimonie of Antiquitie (? 1567).

His intention at that time was 'to have the use of them for a tyme. Meaninge with thankes shorttlye to returne them again'.[1]

A little later Parker was making similar enquiries at St David's. His letter to Bishop Davies reveals the interesting fact that already in March 1565/6 he had got together 'divers books and works' in Anglo-Saxon and had in his house scholars well able to understand them.[2] His task of collecting the books needed for his purpose must have been completed in this year, for in the Preface to his *Testimonie of Antiquitie*, published probably in 1567,[3] he mentions Anglo-Saxon manuscripts 'yet reserved in the libraryes of... Worceter, Hereford, and Exeter' and adds: 'From which places diverse of these bookes have bene delivered into the handes of the moste reverend father, Matthewe, Archbyshop of Canterburye...'.

Amongst the scholars whom Parker speaks of as being in his house must have been John Joscelyn, his Latin secretary, who held a prebend in Hereford Cathedral between 1560 and 1577. That Joscelyn was in touch with the library at Worcester is shown by the fact that it is from him that we learn that the Worcester Saxon Chronicle, now B.M. Cotton Tiberius B. iv, was still in the library of that Church ('est adhuc in bibliotheca ecclesiæ') in his day, at some time, as has been shown, between 1560 and 1567.[4] And it was probably at Worcester during these years that he began to make use of this Chronicle. To the same period must be assigned the annotations which he made in so many of the more ancient Worcester manuscripts, for his hand occurs not only in those which left the library in the sixteenth century but also in those which remained there until the seventeenth.[5] The manuscripts he used for his Anglo-Saxon word-lists in Lambeth Palace MS. 692 include five from Worcester, namely Bodleian, Hatton 20, 113, Junius 121, and Corpus Christi College, Cambridge, 178 and 198. The same three Bodleian manuscripts and Corpus Christi College, Cambridge, 265 supplied copy for Joscelyn's collectanea in Cotton Vitellius D. vii. These collectanea contain also at f. 129 extracts from a 'Vita S. Goaris'[6] of

---

[1] The letter is printed in full by its discoverer, B. H. Streeter, *The Chained Library* (London 1931), p. 347. The books which the Hereford Chapter sent were 'Vita Sancti Marcelini', 'Sermones dominicales' and 'Vite quorundam sanctorum saxonice script.'.

[2] *Correspondence of Matthew Parker* (Parker Soc. 1853): Bishop Davies of St David's to Archbishop Parker, 19 March 1565/6; Archbishop Parker to Bishop Davies, 28 March 1566.

[3] Strype (*op. cit.* 1, 472) dates the work 1566 and states that the Preface is undoubtedly Parker's work.

[4] Ivor Atkins, 'Origin of later part of Saxon Chronicle known as D', *English Historical Review*, vol. LV (1940), p. 25.

[5] Joscelyn wrote in twelve Worcester manuscripts: Bodleian, Hatton 20, 113, 114, Junius 121, Laud misc. 482, Rawlinson C. 428; C.C.C., Cambridge, 9, 198, 265; B.M., Cotton Tiberius A. xiii, Tiberius B. iv, Nero E. 1. Archbishop Parker's red-pencil notes and interlining occur in Hatton 42, Junius 121 and Rawlinson C. 428.

[6] This saint is commemorated at 6 July in the Kalendar of St Wulstan's Homiliary (MS. Hatton 113).

which it is noted 'Habetur in lib. Wigorniensis bibliothecæ', and at ff. 146–7ᵛ a fragment of a Middle-English text on the translation of the scriptures into the vernacular, copied 'out of a boke which remayneth in the Librarye of Worcester'. No copy of a life of St Goar coming from Worcester is now known to exist. The fate of the Middle-English text is known from a note by Wanley opposite the description of Vitellius D. vii in a Bodleian copy of Thomas Smith's *Catalogus librorum MSS. bibliothecæ Cottonianæ* (1696).[1] Wanley notes 'Originale extat in Cod. Otho C. 16'. The reference is to one of the badly burnt Cotton manuscripts which, according to Smith's catalogue, formerly contained as art. 6 (ff. 136–40) 'a sermon in defence of the Scripture, in English. Fragmentum'. None of this sermon is now legible in the original manuscript, but it exists in several sixteenth-century copies which testify to the interest it aroused in Archbishop Parker's circle. Two of these copies are among the Archbishop's manuscripts in Corpus Christi College, Cambridge, MS. 100, p. 227 and MS. 298, each of them being headed: 'Hec extracta sunt ex quodam lacero fragmento Bibliothece Wigorn.'. The sermon was apt material for John Foxe, the martyrologist, who used it in his *Acts and Monuments* and noted that his copy of the Worcester manuscript was obtained from Parker (*A.M.*, ed. 1870, III, 202): this copy is now in Foxe's collectanea in the British Museum, Harley MS. 425, ff. 1, 2. Yet another copy, made in the seventeenth century, occurs in a volume of Henry Wharton's collectanea, Lambeth Palace MS. 594, f. 57, this time with the accompanying note 'ex codice MS. Ecclesiæ collegiatæ Westmonasteriensis'. The unexpected reference to the Westminster library is explained by entries in two of the three seventeenth-century Westminster catalogues, which record half a dozen volumes now in the Cotton collection, among them Cotton Otho C. xvi.[2] Thus the Lambeth copy provides the conclusive evidence that Wanley correctly identified the now burnt text in the Otho manuscript with Joscelyn's 'boke which remayneth in the librarye of Worcester'.[3]

Whatever the precise method of alienation we can be sure that a feeling of laxity had descended upon those responsible for the library and its treasures. Thus, on 21 February 1565/6, the then dean (John

[1] Bodleian, Gough London 54, p. 92.

[2] These volumes seem to have formed part of the Westminster collection during much of the seventeenth century (see Robinson and James, *op. cit.* pp. 34–9, 50–2). They were transferred to the Cotton library before 1695, the year of the Westminster fire, and placed at the ends of the Otho C and Otho D shelves. The contents of both shelves were badly injured in the 1731 fire and of the 214 leaves of Otho C. xvi only 102 now remain. There is no evidence that any part of it except ff. 136–40 came from Worcester: these five leaves were probably torn out of a larger book.

[3] The sermon has been printed recently by C. Bühler in *Medium Ævum*, VII (1938), 167, from two fifteenth-century manuscripts which were not known, apparently, to Parker, with collation of four of the five copies of the lost Worcester manuscript. It is printed, also, from a fifteenth-century manuscript by Miss M. Deanesly, *The Lollard Bible* (1920), p. 439, who ascribes it to John Purvey. The fifteenth-century copies are complete: the first 115 lines of Bühler's text were missing in the Worcester manuscript.

Pedder, 1559–?70) showed himself so little mindful of his duties as guardian of Cathedral property that he made a gift of one of its early manuscripts, the 'Cosmographia' of Ethicus, to that remarkable man, Dr John Dee. The book is now B.M. Cotton Vespasian B. x, and its inscription 'Joannes Dee 1565 Februarii 21 Wigorniae ex dono Decani Ecclesiæ Mr. Peddar' starkly records the transaction. That it really was a Cathedral book is vouched for by the fact that it was seen by Leland when he visited Worcester some twenty or thirty years before. How far Dean Pedder's generosity in giving away the Cathedral's books extended we do not know, but it would probably be unfair to limit it to this recorded instance.

Our information about the fate of Worcester books between the time of Parker and the coming of Patrick Young in 1622 or 1623 is extremely scanty. Hemming's famous cartulary, Cotton Tiberius A. xiii, bears on an end-leaf the name of John Alderford of Abbots Salford.[1] B.M. Cotton Otho C. I, part 2, an Anglo-Saxon version of the dialogues of Pope Gregory, bears at the foot of f. 31 'Michael Lapworthus medicus Novemb. 1593'.[2] Joscelyn had in his possession an Anglo-Saxon chronicle, probably Cotton Tiberius B. iv (The Worcester Chronicle), in view of the number of annotations in his hand in this manuscript.[3] Such Worcester books as Cotton owned do not seem, therefore, to have come to him direct from Worcester. Bodleian MS. Auct. F. 1. 9 (*S.C.* 4137), a miscellaneous volume of the twelfth century containing *inter alia* works by Robert de Losinga, bishop of Hereford, the friend of St Wulstan, and by Walcher, prior of Great Malvern (the first datable 1086, the second 1107–12), belonged to Hatton, but, though certainly a Worcester book, it is not to be counted as part of his spoils since it is not found in Young's catalogue. The manuscript contains the name of William Riggs as owner in the sixteenth century.

Towards the close of the sixteenth century the library seems to have been in the care of William Thornhill, who came of a Yorkshire family and held the eighth prebendal stall in Worcester Cathedral from 1584 to 1626. His connection with the library began shortly after his coming to Worcester, and various inscriptions found in Worcester manuscripts now in the Royal library and in the Bodleian suggest that from time to time he allowed books to leave the Worcester library on loan. He was careful, however, to insert in each book an inscription testifying that it was the property of the Church of Worcester. Seven Worcester manuscripts bearing such inscriptions are known. Four passed to the Royal

---

[1] Alderford died 27 December 1606 and is buried at Salford Priors, Warwickshire. His marriage to Elizabeth Dormer, widow, daughter of Peter Dormer of Newbottle in Northamptonshire, 6 July 1579, is recorded on f. 197 of Hemming's cartulary.

[2] Michael Lapworth, fellow of All Souls College 1562, M.B. 1573, probably father of Edward Lapworth (1574–1636: see *D.N.B.*). The family is of Sowe in Warwickshire.

[3] Amongst Cotton's notes of book-loans (Harley MS. 6018, f. 156) he records 'Old Saxon story manuscrip. It was Mr Gocelins'.

library, three to the Bodleian.[1] All four of the Royal group were at
Worcester in Young's time and were included in his catalogue.[2] At the
time of Young's visit Thornhill was an old man. Indeed, he had been
a prebendary for about forty years. It is likely therefore that when
Young took these manuscripts into his hands they already bore the
inscriptions which we see in them to-day, and that after having been
lent out by Thornhill towards the end of the sixteenth century the
volumes had returned to the library only to await their final dispersal
some twenty years after Young had examined them.

Three of Thornhill's inscriptions bearing a date may be reproduced
in full. The first, in Royal 2 D. xxvi, reads: '16 Dec. 1586, liber ecce
Ecclesiæ beatæ Mariæ Wigorn. teste Guil. Thornhill Eboracensi, ejusdem
Eccl. prebendario octavo'. The second, in Bodley 861, reads: 'Liber
librarii Wigorniensis inde desumptus Mar. 22 1590 et illuc restituendus'.
The third, found in Bodley 113, a fifteenth-century Sarum Hours of the
Virgin, is especially interesting.[3] It reads: 'Hunc librum inveni in cista
Henrici Himbleton et inde accepi June 13 1588, G. Thornhill'. This
Book of Hours, which thus escaped the destruction which befell the
old service-books during the reign of Edward VI, was probably kept
by Himbleton in a box in the sacrist's stall.[4]

At least nine Worcester manuscripts reached the Bodleian in mysteri-
ous circumstances early in the seventeenth century.[5] Their presence
is first recorded by Thomas James in the list of accessions between 1605
and 1611 contained in MS. Bodley 510 (S.C. 2569). They include a
number of uncommon and interesting texts. One of them, Bodley 861,
was removed from Worcester in 1590 (see above).

Towards the middle of the seventeenth century three men become
prominently associated with Worcester's literary history: William
Dugdale (1605–1686) the antiquary, Christopher, first Baron Hatton
(?1605–1670), and John Theyer (1597–1673), a lawyer who amassed
a large collection of manuscripts.

Dugdale was perhaps first on the scene. His quest for materials for
his *Antiquities of Warwickshire* and for the *Monasticon* brought him to
Worcester in 1640, 1643 and 1644, and he may have been there in
other years. He appears to have been at the Cathedral in 1640, for
the account of Worcester monastery in the *Monasticon* opens with a

---

[1] Royal 2 D. xxvi, 2 E. xi, 2 F. 1, 3 A. viii; Bodl. 113 (S.C. 1971), 861 (S.C. 2728),
Auct. D. inf. 2. 4 (S.C. 4089).

[2] Nos. 6, 61, 67 and 59.

[3] The manuscript was probably acquired by the Bodleian between 1613 and 1620.

[4] Himbleton was present as a monk at the election of Holbeche, the last prior,
in 1535. In 1541 he became a minor canon in the New Foundation. He was sacrist
1558–87 (Noake, *Monastery*, pp. 541–4) and probably to his death in 1588. His name,
spelt Hymmulton, is scribbled in the Worcester manuscripts F. 64 and F. 76.

[5] MSS. Auct. F. 5. 16, Auct. F. inf. 1. 3, Bodley 81, 442, 633, 692, 828, 861, 868
(S.C. 2581, 2747, 2269, 2383, 1966, 2508, 2695, 2728, 2749). MS. Bodley 543 (S.C. 2588)
may be from Worcester.

quotation from a Register which is cited as being at Worcester in that year.[1] In 1643 he made a long stay in the city. In July he was engaged upon a systematic examination of the long series of Registers of the bishops of Worcester, from which he made many and lengthy extracts;[2] a month later he was at the Cathedral, calendaring the charters still remaining in the possession of the dean and Chapter. It is interesting to notice that this index of ninety-two charters which he then made and dated 4 August 1643[3] does not include the fifteen Worcester charters now in the British Museum which are known to have been at one time in Lord Hatton's possession.[4] This highly important group of charters must therefore have passed out of the Chapter's keeping before that time. Our authority for Dugdale's presence in Worcester in 1644 is Anthony Wood.[5]

Lord Hatton's connection with Worcester must next be considered. Unfortunately we know nothing of his Worcester contacts. In the early 1640's he and Dugdale were together at Oxford, whither they had accompanied King Charles. From 1643 to 1646, while the King was at Oxford, Hatton was controller of the Royal household. It seems likely, then, that Lord Hatton came to Worcester from Oxford, possibly in company with Dugdale, on some occasion or occasions between 1640 and 1644. Before 4 August 1643, as we have seen, he had acquired the charters already alluded to, and some time before August 1644 he had persuaded the dean and Chapter to allow him to borrow and remove from Worcester the famous group of manuscripts now associated with his name.[6] The subsequent history of these manuscripts will be discussed later.

Theyer's connection with Worcester is made notable by the fact that

---

[1] *Monasticon Anglicanum* (ed. 1817), I, 584: 'Ex Registro quodam penes Decanum et Capitulum Ecclesiæ Cath. Wigorniæ A. 1640'.

[2] The extracts from the Registers are in Bodleian MS. Dugdale 9 (*S.C.* 6499).

[3] Dugdale's list of the charters was printed by Hickes, *Institutiones Grammaticæ* (1689), pt. 2, p. 169, and by Wanley, *Catalogus Librorum Veterum Septentrionalium* (vol. 2 of Hickes's *Thesaurus*, 1705), p. 299, from a very faulty copy. It is unfortunate that C. H. Turner, *Early Worcester Manuscripts* (1916), pp. xxxii–xxxix, followed the printed editions and not Dugdale's autograph, now Bodleian MS. Dugdale 12 (*S.C.* 6502), p. 502.

[4] Now Add. Ch. 19788–19802 (*B.M. Catalogue of Additions to the Manuscripts*, 1854–75, II, 803), acquired in 1873 from Lord Winchilsea into whose family they came by the marriage of Anne, daughter of the second Lord Hatton, with Daniel Finch, sixth Lord Winchilsea.

[5] Wood, *Athen. Ox.* (1691–2), II, 695.

[6] Both the acquisition of the charters and the loan of the manuscripts may have been negotiated by Dugdale. The latter was working in close touch with Lord Hatton and was under great obligations to him. Indeed, it was Lord Hatton's liberality that enabled Dugdale to undertake the completion of the *Antiquities of Warwickshire*. By August 1644 the manuscripts had been removed to Oxford, where they were used by Dugdale that year in the compilation of his Anglo-Saxon dictionary (Dugdale MS. 29, *S.C.* 6519). Bodleian MS. Hatton 114 was indexed by Dugdale 5 August 1644: Hatton 113 on 12 August 1644.

some time before the middle of the seventeenth century he had acquired from the Cathedral library a considerable body of the finest manuscripts then remaining. Nothing is known of the circumstances under which he obtained them.[1]

After Dugdale's visit in August 1643, the dean and Chapter, realizing that events were moving swiftly towards possible disaster, took such action as was in their power to ensure the safety of their muniments. In the following November they granted to Francis Streete, their steward, the use and custody during his life of the great tower over the gate (i.e. the Edgar Tower) for the putting in order and better preservation of the records of their church.

Three years later, 24 July 1646, the city surrendered to Parliament. The sequestration of the Cathedral and city clergy followed immediately, the Committee of Sequestrations taking possession of the prebendal houses and other cathedral property. The Parliamentary Survey of 1649 indeed shows that one of these houses,[2] that held by Dr William Smyth, was at once seized by the County Committee and granted and leased to 'John Seaverne gent.', rent free, 'in regard of his keeping the Library of the Cathedral'.[3] Seaverne[4] seems to have obtained possession before the summer of 1646 was over. This fact is of great significance, for it shows that the care of the library passed at once from the Chapter to the Committee upon whom Parliament had thrown responsibility for the preservation of property. We have some reason, therefore, to suppose that the library was well cared for during the Commonwealth. Seaverne, or Severne as the name was generally spelt, came of a well-known Worcestershire family and was a man of independent means. He had been living in the parish of St Michael since 1634, perhaps in the house of Dr N. Gyles, prebendary of the fifth stall.[5] In 1648 his daughter Katherine married John Somers, a Worcester attorney, who had fought on the side of the Parliamentarians. One of their children, John, was the future Lord Chancellor. John Severne the elder died 13 April 1660. He appears to have had the keeping of the library from 1646 to the time of his death.

At the Restoration the Cathedral and everything connected with it became matters of loving care to the new treasurer, the saintly Barnabas

---

[1] The matter is discussed further on pp. 17–18.

[2] The house attached to the first stall. See, for its position, *infra*, p. 23.

[3] *Parliamentary Survey of Lands and possessions of the Dean and Chapter of Worcester made in or about the year* 1649 (Worcestershire Hist. Soc., 1924). The survey of the College (Cathedral) was made in June (p. 169). A description is given (pp. 174–5) of the house and garden leased by the Committee of Sequestrations to John Seaverne. The terms of the lease end with the words: 'All which he hath held for 3 years past, in regard of his keeping the Library of the Cathedral, without paying any other rent therefore'.

[4] He was born at Powick near Worcester in 1588. In 1634 he lost two of his daughters as victims of the plague which then raged in the city. One of them was buried 'out of Dr Giles howse in the colledge' (St Michael's Register).

[5] This house, which was destroyed in 1851, stood below the west front of the Cathedral, on the site of the infirmary of the monastery.

Oley,[1] a man to whom the Cathedral owes a greater debt than has yet been measured for the part he took in making good its wasted fabric and in quickening its spiritual life when that life was at its lowest ebb. Though he may not have been specially interested in the library Oley was concerned about the losses of important manuscripts which it was known to have sustained. Towards the end of 1666 he approached the great antiquary, Sir William Dugdale, about the matter. He had been negotiating with Dugdale about collecting the ledgers and other 'Church Evidences' which had been sent to London for safety during the period of the Commonwealth, probably on the instructions of the County Committee. These Dugdale had got together and for his services had received from the Chapter the sum of five pounds, no inconsiderable amount in those days.[2] In the course of their correspondence Oley seems to have questioned Dugdale about the fate of the Anglo-Saxon manuscripts whose disappearance he knew was associated with Lord Hatton, if not with Dugdale himself. Dugdale's memory of events leading to the removal of the manuscripts from Worcester must have been very much fresher than his reply suggests. He wrote vaguely and guardedly:

(SIR WILLIAM DUGDALE to PREBENDARY BARNABAS OLEY, 26 January 1666/7)

...I do very well remember those old manuscripts wh. do belong to your Church of Worcester, that were borrowed by the Lord you meane; and are (sic) confident that they are safe, wch I doubt they would hardly have been, in case they had continued at Worcester. There were many other old manuscripts there, wch I then saw, I wish y^t they be not destroyed in these late confusions, or stolen.

As for these, if I have the good hop to see you in London in Easter Term next...I shall then direct you how to obtain them again....

Oley's note at the foot, dated 25 March 1667, reads:

The Lord Hatton is the Ld above intimated. the manuscripts are of some Saxon Homeles. Enquire of Dr. Bolton P^rbend of Westminster.[3]

Oley's reference is to the first Lord Hatton, who did not die until three

---

[1] Barnabas Oley (1602–1686), fellow, and some time president of Clare College, Cambridge. A Royalist, he was prebendary of Worcester, 1660–86, and vicar of Great Gransden in Huntingdonshire. He edited George Herbert's *Remains*, 1652 (*D.N.B.*).

[2] A. lxiii, f. 68. This was not the first batch of documents that had been recovered. In 1661 Oley had paid £1. 17s. od. 'for carrying five boxes of evidences from London'. The 'evidences' probably consisted of the Registers and Ledgers connected with the offices of the Treasurer and Receiver-General, together with other documents concerned with the Cathedral property.

[3] These portions of Dugdale's letter were printed in Maggs's *Catalogue* 449 (1924), p. 113. The letter was written from 'Blythe Hall, neare Coleshill'. Samuel Bolton, D.D., was chaplain in ordinary to Charles II. He died in 1669, 'a man of extraordinary ability and great integrity' (*D.N.B.*).

years later. The manuscripts of 'Saxon Homeles' are no doubt now Hatton 113, 114, 115 and 116. These form, however, only part of Lord Hatton's acquisitions from Worcester. The important manuscripts Hatton 76, Junius 121 and Hatton 20 also belong to the Anglo-Saxon group. Hatton 93 (Young no. 223) is a 'De officio misse' in Anglo-Saxon script of s. viii/ix. Hatton 23 (Y. 222), of the mid-eleventh century, is the earliest extant copy of Cassian's 'Collationes' written in England. Hatton 30[1] and 42 (Y. 24 and 221) contain inscriptions connecting them with St Dunstan. Hatton 6 (Y. 324) is a magnificent wide-margined legal book of the late twelfth century. Hatton 48 (Y. 216) is the eighth-century uncial Rule of St Benedict.

None of these manuscripts returned to Worcester. All, in the end, passed to the Bodleian. Yet on the evidence it is clear that Lord Hatton had no right to retain them in his keeping. Dugdale's letter to Barnabas Oley shows that he had no doubt in his mind that the volumes were not Hatton's property. But though the latter was still alive it was no doubt difficult for Dugdale to approach his benefactor about so delicate a matter as the restoration of the manuscripts to Worcester.[2] Oley himself must have had the facts from the two senior prebendaries, Nathaniel Tomkins and Giles Thornborough, who had taken a prominent part in Chapter affairs since 1629. Lord Hatton used to be credited with having presented the Worcester manuscripts to the Bodleian.[3] But this was not the case. At his death (4 July 1670) all the Worcester volumes, except four which his son retained, were sold, with the rest of Lord Hatton's library, to Robert Scot the London bookseller. Within a very short time Scot sold them to the Bodleian and they came to that library in 1671. The four books which the second Lord Hatton kept back he presented to the Bodleian in 1675.[4] The gift was suitably acknowledged at the time; indeed we find it recorded to-day in the account which the *Dictionary of National Biography* gives of the second lord. This is as far as we can get, at present, in the story of the alienation of these Worcester books.

Turning to the other group of manuscripts which disappeared from Worcester about the middle of the seventeenth century, it is difficult to explain how John Theyer got possession of the twenty-five Worcester books which, with the rest of his collection, passed by purchase into the

[1] See note, p. 80.
[2] An entry in Anthony Wood's Diary corroborates Dugdale's view. Under October 1687 we find an inserted slip, apparently in Obadiah Walker's hand: 'Quaere in whose hands a vol. of Saxon Homilies belonging formerly to the church of Worcester and lent to my Lord Hatton' (Wood's *Life and Times*, ed. A. Clark, III, 239).
[3] Macray, *Annals of the Bodleian Library* (1868), pp. 99–100 and 327.
[4] These are now Hatton 113, 114, 115 and 116. Another Worcester book came to the Bodleian later. Junius 121, though included in the Hatton books bought by Scot, was sold by Scot to John Fell, afterwards bishop of Oxford (1675–86), apparently before the sale of the Hatton collection to the Bodleian in 1671. Fell gave it to the Bodleian probably between 1675 and 1686. See the account in *Summary Catalogue*, No. 5232, and in Wood's *Life and Times*, III, 239 and note.

Royal library in 1678. Theyer had been educated at Magdalen College, Oxford, and after leaving Oxford went to London to take up the study of law. But he did not long remain there, preferring to return to his patrimony at Cooper's Hill, Brockworth, Gloucestershire, in order to devote himself to his books. In 1643 he was created M.A. at the request of the King. Anthony Wood, who spent a week with him in September 1668, describes Cooper's Hill as a 'Lone-house' and says that his friend had a fine collection of manuscripts 'repos'd in a Roome which he had built to retaine them'. Elsewhere Wood tells us that Theyer was a zealous Royalist and that he had suffered much in the Civil War. Worcester must have been easy of access to Theyer and he was probably well aware of what was going on there, but the circumstances under which he was allowed to get possession of so many valuable manuscripts are difficult to understand. The mere shelf-room which these books occupied must have been considerable, so that it is clear that they could not have been removed without the knowledge of those responsible for them. The Chapter Act Books extend to 1645 but contain no reference to the manuscripts after 1625. The only conclusion to be drawn would seem to be that Theyer acquired them legitimately and by purchase. This may have been between 1644 and 1646.[1]

These Theyer manuscripts appear to represent the cream of what was left in the library about the middle of the seventeenth century. Royal 4 A. xiv (Young no. 5) is written in beautiful Anglo-Saxon minuscule of the tenth century. Royal 5 E. xiii (Y. 333) is a ninth-century continental manuscript. Royal 5 F. iii (Y. 253), of the ninth century, is one of the two oldest copies of Aldhelm's 'De laude virginitatis' written in England. Royal 15 A. xxxiii (Y. 305), of the tenth century, contains commentaries on the 'De nuptiis' of Martianus, and belonged to the monastery of St Remi at Rheims at an early date.[2] It was one of the books noticed by Leland at Worcester. A large number of these Theyer manuscripts consist of the twelfth-century patristic and biblical works which formed the foundation stock of most monastic libraries, and which are so notably lacking at Worcester to-day. Last in order, because it cannot be identified quite certainly with Young no. 309, but first in age and importance, is the eighth-century 'libellus precum', Royal 2 A. xx.[3]

[1] A fiercely Royalist note in Theyer's hand in Royal 2 A. xx is dated 15 July 1649. Royal 3 A. viii bears the name of Francis Ash as owner in 1647. This is probably the 'Mr Ash of Worcester' from whom Sir Symon Archer had 'a Booke of the Tenures of Worcestershire' (letter dated 5 Nov. 1650 in *Life of Sir William Dugdale*, ed. by Hamper, 1827).

[2] For the close connection between the monasteries of St Remi and Worcester about the end of the eleventh century cf. Ivor Atkins, 'The Church of Worcester from the eighth to the twelfth century', *Antiquaries Journal*, xx (1940), 37.

[3] The probability that Royal 2 A. xx is identical with Young no. 309 is strengthened by the fact that all other Theyer manuscripts of earlier date than the twelfth century come from Worcester, except Royal 8 B. xi. All Hatton manuscripts older than the twelfth century come from Worcester, except Hatton 43.

Three more manuscripts which disappeared from the library between 1623 and 1697 remain to be noticed.

The first, a Bodleian manuscript, Barlow 4, s. xi, which came to the Bodleian with Bishop Barlow's collection in 1691,[1] is one of two known English copies of the 'Liber Comitis' of Smaragdus—the other being still at Worcester (MS. F. 91). That Barlow 4 is a Worcester book is certain both from the character of the script and decoration of the first leaves (s. xi *ex.*), and from the fact that the name 'Thomas Grene' scribbled on a flyleaf (s. xv) occurs again in the same hand in Worcester Cathedral MS. Q. 17. The manuscript has a general resemblance to the set of three great homiliaries remaining at Worcester (F. 92–4).

The second, Eton College MS. 96, 'Petri Pictavensis compendium veteris testamenti', has good claim to be identified with Young no. 342, since it measures $18\frac{1}{2} \times 13\frac{3}{4}$ inches and so answers very well to Young's 'fol. large'. It contains, moreover, a short chronicle extending to A.D. 1241 added to the compendium of Peter of Poitiers, which fits well with Young's description 'usque ad annum 1242'. The name 'Elizabeth Flobern' (or more probably 'Flovern'), in a seventeenth-century hand, is found on f. 7. The manuscript seems to have reached Eton after 1697, since it is not included in Bernard's catalogue.

The third, Glasgow, Hunterian V. 5. 1, is a copy of the 'Regula Pastoralis' of St Gregory the Great, partly (ff. 1–101) of the late tenth or early eleventh century, and partly (ff. 102–57) of the twelfth century. There can be no question about its being a Worcester book, for it contains marginalia which are unmistakably in the well-known 'tremulous' Worcester hand.[2] It is likely therefore to be one of two copies of 'Pastorale Gregorii' listed by Young—either Y. 37 or Y. 38.[3]

We have seen that in writing to Barnabas Oley in January 1666/7 Dugdale expressed his fear lest the manuscripts which he had seen at Worcester should have been destroyed or stolen during the troubles and confusions of the Civil War.[4] Towards the end of his life these

---

[1] It may be significant that Thomas Barlow was a prebendary of Worcester, 1660–76. He was afterwards bishop of Lincoln.

[2] The hand is that of a late-twelfth or early-thirteenth-century Worcester monk whose glosses have done much to establish the Worcester provenance of Anglo-Saxon manuscripts now scattered through the great libraries, which otherwise must have passed unrecognized as Worcester books. Of the numerous manuscripts in which this hand occurs the only one now at Worcester consists of fragments of Ælfric's Grammar and of two Early Middle English verse pieces, found by Sir Thomas Phillipps in 1837 'in the cover of an old book', 'among the archives of Worcester Cathedral', and now bound up as F. 174. These leaves are entirely in the 'tremulous' hand. See also Turner, *Early Worcester Manuscripts* (1916), p. lvi.

[3] The older part of the manuscript was copied from an exemplar in Insular (Irish or Welsh) minuscule, as appears from the abbreviations and from the incorrect expansion of abbreviations peculiar to the Insular script, e.g. *etin* for *etiam*, *si* for *sicut* (Irish or Welsh *etī*, *s^i*) and frequent *tunc* for *tamen*, due apparently to misunderstanding of the Insular abbreviation *tn̄* for *tamen*. A Welsh gloss, 'duglas', is in the margin of f. 136ᵛ, opposite 'ceruleus' in the text.

[4] *Vide supra*, p. 16.

fears had strengthened to the conviction, expressed in his *Short view of the late Troubles in England* (published in 1681), that Essex's army in September 1642 'rifled the Library with the Records and Evidences of the Church' and 'tore in pieces the Bibles and Service-books pertaining to the Quire'.[1] While this statement may be true of the service-books— no doubt printed books, which may well have been easily accessible to the soldiery—it is less likely to be true of the charters, which at this time were stored in the Edgar Tower. As to the library, there are good grounds for thinking that Dugdale was mistaken in his charge. At this time it was housed, as we shall see, in the triforium of the south aisle of the nave, and being protected above and below by doors was more or less inaccessible.

But the real challenge to Dugdale's statement comes from the evidence of the work which lies before us. From it we learn, for the first time, what manuscripts the library of Worcester possessed before the Civil War and we are forced to the conclusion that the Parliamentary soldiers took little, if any, direct part in despoiling the library. The grievous losses suffered between 1623 and 1697 were due in fact rather to the studied selection and withdrawal of the choicest manuscripts by scholars and collectors than to haphazard destruction wrought by soldiers.

At the same time there are losses which cannot be accounted for, and which may be, but more probably are not, due to the troubles of the time. Young lists twenty-six manuscripts which are not to be found in any of the subsequent catalogues and which have not been traced to other libraries.[2] Of these Young nos. 20 and 21 are described as 'vetus', no. 54 contained a collection of admonitions for parish priests, 'charactere Saxonico', no. 23 a bestiary and the rare disputation between Pippin and Alcuin, and no. 337 two sermons in Anglo-Saxon and the fables of Æsop in the version of Romulus. In addition to these twenty-six there are several entries in Young's catalogue which cannot be identified with certainty, the descriptions being too brief or too general. Whether Lord Somers (1651–1716) was able to obtain possession of any of the Cathedral's manuscript books we do not know. Charters he did get, to the number of twenty-four out of the ninety-two which had been seen by Dugdale in 1643. These twenty-four, described by Wanley when they were in Somers's possession,[3] were printed, by good luck, in the appendix to Dr John Smith's edition of the Anglo-Saxon Bede. None of them is known to exist now, and it is supposed that they were destroyed, with Somers's papers, in a fire in Lincoln's Inn in 1752. On the other hand, Somers's manuscript books passed to Sir Joseph Jekyll and were sold by auction in 1739/40. The sale catalogue does not list any manuscript which is likely to be from Worcester.

Even in comparatively recent times manuscripts have disappeared, though their loss has to some extent been compensated for by later

[1] p. 557.   [2] *Vide supra*, pp. 5–7.   [3] Wanley, *op. cit.* p. 301.

acquisitions.[1] Ten manuscripts, described in 1697, nine of them medieval and one Chinese (called simply 'Manuscriptus Codex Sinensis'), are no longer at Worcester.[2] It is probably significant that they were all quartos. One of them, no. 218 in Young's catalogue (Q. 25 in that of 1697), a volume containing 'multe compilaciones', letters of Peter of Blois and a life of St Modwenna, is now Royal 15 B. iv. The compilers of the *Catalogue of Royal and King's Manuscripts in the British Museum* were unable to trace the history of this manuscript, which is not recorded in the old Royal library lists. It was described, however, in Casley's catalogue and so must have reached the Royal library before 1734. A second, Young no. 286 (Q. 57 in 1697 catalogue), is now B.M. Harley 5394. It is a miscellaneous volume, written in the fourteenth century, containing, amongst other matter, the Life of Barlaam and Josaphat. A third and fourth, catalogued separately as Q. 38 and Q. 80 in 1697, appear to be now bound up together in Harley 4967. Q. 38, a legal manuscript, is Young no. 167. Q. 80, containing various classical and grammatical texts, is not recorded by Young. Both Harleian manuscripts (nos. 5394 and 4967) were catalogued by Casley *c.* 1736.

Young's catalogue was compiled eighty years after the dissolution of the monastery. The analogy of some other Cathedral collections would suggest that the intervening period is likely to have produced a certain number of gifts of manuscripts. John Bridges gave manuscripts to the library at Winchester in the early seventeenth century. At Lincoln and Hereford a number of books were acquired from local monastic houses. But at Worcester, as at Durham, there is no evidence that the library received additions in this period. One of the few books known to have belonged to another monastic house is F. 150 (apparently Young no. 188), which came from St Dogmael's, Pembrokeshire, a Benedictine abbey. F. 33 belonged in the sixteenth century to a 'Mastur of Chapell' named Thomas Compton. Q. 10 (Young no. 75) contains the name 'Frauncis Dingley' and the date 1617.[3] On the whole it seems likely that a few, but only a few, books were added to the library between 1540 and 1623.

It will be well to say something about the housing of the library at different stages of its history.

From the twelfth to the last quarter of the seventeenth century the library appears to have occupied a position over the south aisle of the nave. At first, from the twelfth to about the end of the fourteenth century, it was housed 'chiefly in a room....over the south aisle at the extreme west of the cathedral church [that is, in what is now the ante-

---

[1] See Appendix V.

[2] 1697 catalogue, Q. 18, 25, 32, 38, 57, 58, 73, 78, and 80. The Chinese manuscript is no. 81. The contents of these manuscripts are set out in the 1906 catalogue on pp. 173 and 174. Four of them, namely Q. 25, 38, 57 and 58, were listed by Young (nos. 218, 167, 286 and 293 of his catalogue).

[3] Francis Dingley of Charlton, Cropthorne, died 27 October 1624. The book would appear to have come to the library between 1617 and 1622/3.

chamber to the present library], and partly in aumbries in the cloister'.[1]
In the latter part of the fourteenth century the whole of the Norman
south side of the nave, with the exception of the two western bays, was
rebuilt. Opportunity was taken to make provision for the library by
the erection of a room extending from the third western bay of the aisle
to the north transept. From the twelfth century onwards the library
was approached from below by a circular stone staircase to which two
doors gave access, the one at the north-west end of a passage in the
north cloister leading to the infirmary, the other within the Cathedral
at the west end of the south aisle of the nave.[2] Through one of these
doors Patrick Young must have passed in 1622 or 1623 when on his
way to view the manuscripts.

About ten years after his visit important changes took place in and
around the Cathedral, some of which have been mistakenly thought
to have affected the safety of the manuscripts during the period of the
Civil War. These changes were brought about by Archbishop Laud's
Visitation of the Cathedral in 1634. We must confine ourselves to those
which affect the library.

There was at this time lying between the north porch and the entrance to the bishop's palace (now the deanery) an old ruined building,
formerly the Capella Carnaria, which had long since been disused.[3]
The Capella Carnaria belonged to the dean and Chapter, but for almost
a hundred years had been let to the bishop for the time being. At the
time of the archbishop's Visitation it was held by the aged Bishop
Thornborough, who made use of it as a hay barn. Indeed the bishop
claimed later that the chapel 'was used by the Bishops for a house to
put hay in ever since the dissolution'.[4]

We can well understand that Archbishop Laud would not be likely
to tolerate such desecration. It was in fact one of the matters which
he brought before the dean and Chapter in the articles of enquiry
addressed to them in his Visitation. Later, on 20 February 1635/6,
he issued certain orders to the Chapter, one of which directed that the

---

[1] J. K. Floyer, Introduction to Floyer and Hamilton, *Catalogue of Worcester Cathedral
Manuscripts* (Worc. Hist. Soc., 1906), p. xi. The aumbries were the recesses in the east
wall of the cloisters which can still be seen. They were lined as cupboards to receive
books.

[2] The oldest plans, e.g. that in Thomas's *Survey of the Cathedral Church of Worcester*
(1737), show only the entrance from the cloisters. The earliest to show both entrances
appears to be that in Murray's *Guide* (1867).

[3] This chapel, built by Bishop William de Blois (1218–36), received its name from
the fact that in its crypt were buried the bones removed from the monks' cemetery at
the time when the Lady Chapel was built on the site of the cemetery, *c.* 1224. About
forty years later the chapel was endowed by Bishop Walter de Cantelupe (1237–66)
as a chantry, the bishop making provision for four chaplains to sing daily masses for
the souls of the departed. Since the Reformation the chapel had been allowed to fall
into complete decay.

[4] Bishop John Thornborough to Archbishop Laud, 13 January 1636/7 (*Cal. of
State Papers (Domestic)*, 1636–7, p. 360). Thornborough died in 1641 at the age of
ninety.

Capella Carnaria, 'now profaned and made a hay-barn be restored and employed to the wonted use'.[1] The Chapter were, no doubt, anxious to carry out this order. But there were difficulties. Although they were in sympathy with Laud's views, especially with those affecting matters of Church order, there were limits beyond which they were not prepared to go in the prosecution of his ideals.

They were unable to see their way to restoring the chapel to its old-time use. The matter was long deliberated. At length, on 29 October 1636, the Chapter arrived at a decision fraught, as it proved, with disastrous results to their relations with the City, bad as these had been for some time. That decision was to move the school from the refectory, where it was splendidly accommodated, to the Capella Carnaria, a building in every way unfit, whether from its position or on account of the entirely inadequate accommodation it could offer, even when reconditioned. It was expressed in a Chapter Order which decreed

[*Acta Capituli*, LXXV, f. 126 *b*]

that the chappell called Capella Carnaria shalbe fitted up for the Scholehouse, and that the Scholehouse that now is shalbe converted into a Librarie, and a dore made thereinto out of the Cloyster, and that, as soone as conveniently may be, parte of the house which is nowe Dr. Steward's shalbe prouided for the Scholemaster.

Dr Steward occupied the house assigned to the first prebendary. This house was built against the west end of the north choir aisle of the Cathedral. In pre-Reformation times it had been the sacrist's lodging and, during the Commonwealth, as we have seen, was granted rent free to John Seaverne in consideration of his keeping the Cathedral library.

To carry out their plan the Chapter immediately proceeded to fit up the Capella Carnaria and to make part of Dr Steward's house suitable as offices for the school. In a short time, to the immense resentment of the citizens, the school was set up in the chapel. Habington in recording the event a little later seems to reflect the general feeling.

...now of late they removed the famous Grammer schole wch hath in this our age byn equal wth the best in England from the place which was once the Refectorie of the monks w^thin the Colledge of Wor[cester] to this chappell of the charnelhouse which is w^thout the cathedral church.[2]

But having established the school in the Capella Carnaria the Chapter paused. Perhaps the removal had been more costly than had been anticipated. Whatever the reason, it is certain that they did not carry

---

[1] *Works of Archbishop Laud* (Library of Anglo-Catholic Theology, 1847–60), v, 481.

[2] From fol. 36 of Worc. Cath. MS. A. xvi, a seventeenth-century transcript of portions of Habington's *Survey of Worcestershire*. This transcript is not amongst the MSS. enumerated in the Worcestershire Historical Society's edition, published in two volumes (I, 1895; II, 1899), from which its readings often differ. See, for example, the passage corresponding to that given above (II, 372).

out their intention to transfer the library from the triforium to the refectory. Hitherto this fact has not been established, but as it has an important bearing upon the history of the manuscripts during the Civil War it will be well to make it clear. That no steps were taken to remove the library is shown by the Dean and Chapter's answer to one of the charges formulated against them by the Mayor and Corporation in a Petition laid before Parliament, and by Parliament referred, 16 February 1640–1, to the bishop of Ely's Committee.[1]

Defending their action in removing the school from the refectory to the Capella Carnaria the dean and Chapter answered that 'the late school [i.e. the Refectory] is designed for our library and a Prebend's house when we are able'. These last words show clearly that up to that time the library had not been moved. Attempts were made to compose the differences between City and Chapter, but a Minute of 29 November, 1641, shows the City Council still unsatisfied. After that date, however, we hear no more of the Petition, and some time in 1642 the school was brought back to the Refectory, the Chapter wisely yielding to the City's demand for its reinstatement.

Throughout the Civil War, then, the manuscripts remained in the chamber over the south aisle of the nave where Young had examined them. The muniments, with the monastic rolls of the Obedientiaries, continued to be housed in the Edgar Tower.[2] It was not until after the Restoration that any change was made in the position of the library. Its removal was considered in 1671 and it was decided that all forfeitures should be spent upon preparing and fitting out the Chapter house as a library.[3]

About May 1675 the books were moved from the south triforium of the nave to the Chapter house, which by then had been made ready to receive the library.[4] In the following year (22 March 1675/6) Dr William Hopkins was installed a prebendary. Hopkins was to take a very active part in the life of the library. An interesting account of his work is given by Dr George Hickes in the Preface which he contributed to a collection of the sermons of Dr Hopkins published in 1708. Hickes, a great Anglo-Saxon scholar, had been dean of Worcester

[1] Worcester Cathedral muniments, D. 312, and entries in Worcester Corporation Minute Book between 18 December 1640 and 29 November 1641 to which Mr Vivian Collett of Worcester kindly drew our attention. For information relating to the Petition we are indebted to Sir Henry Badeley, K.C.B., F.S.A., Clerk of the Parliaments.

[2] In 1635 Dean Mainwaring claimed in a letter to Laud that he had 'preserved thousands of rolls lying in the Tower', removing them 'from a damp stone wall, and from under a window where the rain beat in on them' (*Cal. of State Papers (Domestic)*, 1635, pp. 394–5). Certain of the muniments, e.g. the Church's ledgers, etc., were removed to London during the Commonwealth, probably at the instance of the County Committee.

[3] *Acta Capituli*, 25 November 1671.

[4] The Accounts for 1674/5 show that the books were carried from the old library into the vestry (now St John's chapel) and thence to the Chapter house. This goes to show that they were brought by the door at the west end of the Cathedral.

from 1683 until his ejection as a non-juror in 1691.[1] Of Hopkins's devotion to learning he wrote:

In speaking of his Learning I ought not to forget to tell the World....how much he endeavoured to promote both human and divine Knowledge. Of this he hath left a Proof, and as it were a Monument in the Church of Worcester; I mean the library there, which by his Sollicitation was removed from an inconvenient Place over the South-Isle of the Church into the Chapter-House, a large, beautiful, lightsome and spacious Room, of easier access to the infirm, and much safer for tender Constitutions to spend their Time in.[2]

After the translation of it to that Place, he endeavoured by all means to increase its Stock, and, to that end, with the Dean and Chapter, found ways of raising a constant Supply of Money to buy good Books of all Sorts. He was also wont all my Time to beg Money for it, and by his acquaintance with London-Merchants, procured Books which were rare in England, at easie Rates from Italy, Spain, and France: which so offended our good Friend Mr. Robert Scot of Little Britain, that he was very angry with us, and in his Passion told me he would complain to the King, whose Bookseller he had the Honour to be. I take this occasion to mention that good and worthy Man for his Honour, who for about twenty Years, in many hazardous Voyages successively, brought more good Books, and Learning with them from foreign Parts into England, than perhaps all the English Booksellers for the last hundred Years. But to return to my dear Friend's Mistress, the Library of the Church of Worcester. A little before I left the place, we had procured a fine Collection of the Bibliothecarian Writers of several Countries, with which he was much pleased, and I suppose never left off till he compleated them; and as for the Works of the Greek Fathers, as I remember, they were all in that Library, excepting those of Cyril of Alexandria, which I suppose are since procured. He also took particular care to stock the Library with Writers of the middle Ages, and I doubt not but by this time [1708], if the same care of it hath been continued, it may pass after the publick Libraries in our two famous Universities, for one of the best furnished with printed Books, in the whole Kingdom, as it was with MSS. and ancient Charters before the great Rebellion. And as in his life time he took particular care to furnish and adorn it, so in his last Will and Testament, besides other Charitable Legacies, he gave ten Pounds to buy books for it, thereby testifying how much he desired the Riches of it should always increase.

Hopkins was equally interested in the manuscripts and, as we shall see later, went to considerable trouble in altering their classification, grouping them into two divisions, Folios and Quartos. His system and numbering have been retained to the present time. The result can hardly be described as successful. The old arrangement, as we see it in Young's catalogue, was much more interesting and systematic in

---

[1] Hickes's connection with the Cathedral began in 1680 when he was made a prebendary.

[2] Here, as we have seen, Hickes was in error. The Chapter in 1671 were already taking steps for the removal to the Chapter house. Hopkins did not become a prebendary until 1676.

its grouping, in spite of the fact that from time to time it caused large folios to fraternize in a rather inconvenient way with octavos and quartos. If not ideal, the old arrangement, which may possibly date from medieval times, certainly gave a clearer view of the contents of the collection.

Like Barnabas Oley, Hopkins was concerned about the recovery of the lost manuscripts. A Chapter Minute of June 1687 shows that he was to be 'allowed his expenses in a journey to Oxford to look after some manuscripts belonging to this church'. That visit occupied him from 8 to 13 August. Nothing is known of the result. To the end of his life Hopkins continued to show the same solicitude for everything connected with the library, whether books, manuscripts, or charters. This is shown in Chapter Orders of 1699 directing 'that the rooms over the Porch and Chappel on the north side of this church be fitted up for a Manuscript Library and an Evidence Room'[1] and 'that the Treasurer do pay to Mr Thwayts the sum of £10 towards the charges of printing the charters of this Church'. In the following year Dr Hopkins died, and after his death interest in the library declined. Nothing more appears to have been heard of the work which Edward Thwaites, the Anglo-Saxon scholar (1667–1711), projected. It would be interesting to know whether the materials which he had gathered together are still in existence.[2]

The removal of the library to the Chapter house did not add to the security of its books, still less to that of the manuscripts. In spite of the fact that one of the senior prebendaries, usually the sub-dean, was responsible for the library, the actual administration was generally in the hands of the deputy librarian, who was described as Custos librorum, or Keeper of the Library. In the eighteenth century this office was held by a minor canon or by the headmaster of the school. With the opening of that century came one of the worst periods of neglect in the history of the library. There are constant references in the Act Books to the laxity shown in enforcing such regulations as from time to time had been drawn up to safeguard the books. In a way which the great dean could never have foreseen the Chapter house proved only too easy of access to those who were privileged to use the library. Between the beginning and end of the eighteenth century no fewer than ten of the quartos disappeared. In the last quarter of that century the Rev. John Griffin, headmaster of the King's School, became librarian. He worked enthusiastically and matters gradually improved from his

---

[1] The order relating to the fitting up of rooms over the north porch and Jesus chapel does not appear to have been carried out.

[2] The charters of the Church, for printing of which Thwaites was paid £10, may be those actually printed in Hickes's *Thesaurus* (1705), pp. 139–42, 169–75. Both Hickes and Thwaites were fellows of Queen's College, Oxford, and co-workers on the *Thesaurus*. One of two late-seventeenth-century copies of the same series of charters as that printed by Hickes is in Queen's College, Oxford, MS. 368, pp. 141–70. The other copy is in Harley MS. 4660.

time onward. The Chapter house continued to house the library until 1864, when the restoration of the Cathedral occasioned a temporary removal to the Edgar Tower. There the books remained until 1866, when they were restored to their old home over the south aisle of the nave.

THE LATER SEVENTEENTH-CENTURY CATALOGUES

In the great work which Hopkins accomplished for the library between 1676 and his death in 1700 he had the ardent support of Dr Hickes for eleven years, 1680–91. Both were scholars, both shared a love of Anglo-Saxon studies, both were men of great energy and accustomed to get things done. Hopkins left his mark upon the library in more ways than one. During his time, apparently, two catalogues of the library were produced. The first of these is still in manuscript: the second was printed in 1697 and is known to have been the work of Dr Hopkins.[1] It seems probable that both were his.

The unprinted catalogue is found in Bodleian MS. Tanner 268, where it is one of a collection of catalogues which on internal evidence may be dated about 1675. Occupying folios 113–19 of that manuscript the Worcester example bears the title 'Catalogus Codicum MSS in Bibliotheca Ecclesie Cathedralis Beatæ Mariæ Wigornensis'. Comparison of this catalogue with that compiled by Hopkins in 1697 at once establishes the fact that they are closely related to one another. In Tanner 268 we see for the first time the grouping of the manuscripts into folios and quartos, a system of classification which was again adopted by Hopkins in 1697. The ordering of the volumes within these groups follows the same general scheme in both catalogues, although in Tanner 268 related manuscripts are sometimes separated, perhaps as a result of the lack of familiarity with the collection which one would expect in an early attempt at cataloguing. The impression left upon the mind is that the catalogue was drawn up at the beginning of Dr Hopkins's connection with the library. In 1676 when Hopkins took up work at Worcester he must have found the manuscripts in a very disordered state after their removal to the Chapter house. After setting them out in the new grouping which he had decided to adopt his next step would probably be the provision of a catalogue. Since there does not appear to have been one in existence upon which he could base his work, the cataloguer fell back upon the contents-summaries given on the ancient labels pasted on the covers.[2] The fact that the Tanner catalogue lists only 157 folios and 73 quartos and octavos (here grouped together) against 169 and 82 found in the catalogue of 1697 strengthens the conviction that it represents work done at a very early stage in

[1] Printed in Bernard's *Catalogi MSS. Angliæ et Hiberniæ.*
[2] See Appendix I.

Dr Hopkins's association with the library. On these various grounds we venture to ascribe the Tanner catalogue to him, either directly or indirectly, and to date it *c.* 1676.

This catalogue was known to Floyer when he was preparing the 1906 catalogue, but he does not seem to have made use of it, dismissing it rather summarily as 'an incomplete and very roughly made one'.[1] This is scarcely fair to the catalogue, for while it is true that it is incomplete, the fact that it is almost entirely based, as we have seen, upon the contents lists given on the old labels of the manuscripts themselves makes it of great importance. Indeed, this Tanner catalogue provides what is virtually a late medieval catalogue of the library. It is also valuable historically, for when set beside the catalogue of 1697 it enables us to assess real and apparent losses in the years between.

The Tanner catalogue is interesting, too, for what it reveals of the vagaries of Worcester cataloguing. For incomplete as it is in comparison with that printed in 1697 it enumerates, nevertheless, twelve manuscripts whose presence Hopkins does not record again in 1697. But we should be wrong if we assumed that all these twelve had been lost between *c.* 1676 and 1697. Actually only six disappeared completely; the remaining six reappeared about two hundred and thirty years later in the catalogue of 1906.[2]

Turning to the 1697 catalogue we find that it has for its title 'Librorum Manuscriptorum Ecclesiæ Cathedralis apud Vigorniam Catalogus continens codices CCLII.[3] Hunc autem fecit vir reverendus atque Historiæ Sacræ et Civilis Anglorum peritissimus Guilielmus Hopkins, S.T.P. et Ecclesiæ Wigornensis Canonicus'. It was reprinted at Worcester in 1860. As has already been stated it lists 169 folios and 82 quartos, and is an expanded, and to some extent corrected, recension of the catalogue in Tanner 268. In it Hopkins retains the same general order in the numbering as was adopted in Tanner 268, but modifies it from time to time in order to bring together volumes whose relationship had been previously overlooked. The order which Hopkins finally adopted in 1697 has been retained up to the present time, so that, except for two folios,[4] and for the ten quartos spoken of above as lost in the eighteenth century,[5] all the manuscripts listed in 1697 are to be found in the 1906 catalogue under the same numbers. The missing quarto manuscripts were replaced, apparently at the beginning of the nineteenth century, by others which appear to have escaped Dr Hopkins's

[1] Floyer and Hamilton, *Catalogue of Worcester Cathedral Manuscripts* (Worc. Hist. Soc., 1906), Preface, p. ix.

[2] See Appendix II.

[3] An error. The number should be CCLI.

[4] F. 17 has been missing for many years: the number has not been filled up. F. 95 was reported as missing in 1821 and on p. 47 of the 1906 catalogue it is stated to be no longer in the library, but on p. 173 it is rightly identified with the present Q. 93.

[5] See *ante*, p. 21.

attention. Yet seven of the ten gaps were filled by books which had been included in the catalogue made by Patrick Young.[1] At the same time the 1697 catalogue may include a few ancient Worcester manuscripts which Young failed to list.[2] It shows also the presence of certain manuscripts which had been added to the library between 1676 and 1697.[3]

Between 1781–3 the Rev. John Griffin, then librarian, made catalogues of both the printed books and manuscripts, in two finely-written folio volumes. The 'Catalogus Librorum Manuscriptorum in Bibliotheca Ecclesiae Cathedralis Vigorniae MDCCLXXXI' is found in the second volume. Unfortunately, it proves to be no more than an accurate transcript of the 1697 catalogue. Its chief value lies in the pencilled annotations made by an unknown writer apparently in the early part of the nineteenth century,[4] who notes 'deest' against each of the ten lost quartos and gives a valuable list (also in pencil and extending to a whole folio page) of manuscripts which were still uncatalogued at that time and were stored 'in pluteo 23'.[5] This list is given in Appendix VI.

In 1906 the descriptive catalogue now in use was produced under the editorship of the Rev. J. K. Floyer, a former minor canon and librarian of the Cathedral, and Mr S. G. Hamilton, fellow and librarian of Hertford College, Oxford. It includes some few manuscripts added at the end of the seventeenth and in the course of the eighteenth century,[6] and the list of folios is now extended from F. 170 to 177, and the list of quartos from Q. 82 to 100. There are thus twenty-seven manuscripts added to those described by Hopkins in 1697. But of these twenty-seven manuscripts no fewer than eighteen had already figured in Young's catalogue and they now make their reappearance after having been lost sight of for close upon three hundred years.[7]

---

[1] These seven are Q. 18, 25, 38, 57, 58, 78, 81 of the 1906 catalogue where

| Q. 18 = Y. 312 | Q. 38 = Y. 226 | Q. 58 = Y. 313 | Q. 81 = Y. 269 |
| Q. 25 = Y. 190 | Q. 57 = Y. 239 | Q. 78 = Y. 341 | |

The three remaining gaps were filled with two manuscripts added to the library in the eighteenth century (Q. 73 and Q. 80) and a volume of thirteenth-century fragments (Q. 32) which may have passed unnoticed by Young.

[2] See Appendix IV.

[3] F. 158, 161, 163, 166, Q. 68 and perhaps others.

[4] The annotations were possibly made about 1821, when the contents of the library were being overhauled. See 1906 catalogue, p. 173.

[5] The 1781 catalogue shows that in the arrangement of the manuscripts the folios were placed in plutei 17–21, and the quartos in plutei 22 and 23.

[6] See Appendix V.

[7] They are:

F. 170 = Y. 177	F. 173 = Y. 302?	F. 175 = Y. 210	F. 176 = Y. 154
F. 177 = Y. 212			
Q. 82 = Y. 66	Q. 85 = Y. 246	Q. 87 = Y. 327	Q. 88 = Y. 134
Q. 89 = Y. 299	Q. 90 = Y. 265	Q. 92 = Y. 311	Q. 94 = Y. 68
Q. 96 = Y. 274	Q. 97 = Y. 303	Q. 98 = Y. 228	Q. 99 = Y. 315
Q. 100 = Y. 314?			

CATALOGUS LIBRORUM MANUSCRIPTORUM
BIBLIOTHECAE WIGORNIENSIS

In printing, the spelling and, as far as possible, the punctuation and arrangement of Young's manuscript have been followed, except that:

(1) The modern phonetic distinction in the use of *i* and *j* and of *u* and *v* has been followed. For both *i* and *j* Young uses *i* always initially and medially, but when doubled the second *i* resembles *j*. For both *I* and *J* he uses *J*. For *u* and *v* he uses *v* always initially and *u* always medially.

(2) Quotation marks show the beginning and end of Young's quotations of the opening words of texts.

(3) Interlined words and letters are shown thus, 'civili'.

(4) Young's marginalia and corrections to his text are given in footnotes.

(5) Abbreviations have been expanded, letters not written in Young's manuscript being italicized.

(6) Words and letters omitted in error in Young's manuscript have been added in square brackets.

(7) Identifications with extant manuscripts are added in italics.

(8) The entries are numbered.

(9) Entries marked with an asterisk are discussed in the notes on pp. 63–68.

(10) Dates are given in the following form: 's. xii in.' for early twelfth century, 's. xii med.' for mid-twelfth century, 's. xii ex.' for late twelfth century, 's. xii^1' for first half of the twelfth century, 's. xii^2' for second half of the twelfth century, 's. xii/xiii' for late twelfth or early thirteenth century, 's. xii–xiii' for twelfth and thirteenth centuries.

p. 23, col. 1

1 Chrysos*tomus* in evan*gelium* Johannis cum prologo Burgundionis judicis 'civis Pisani', 'Cum Constantinopoli pro negotiis publicis patriæ meæ a concivibus meis ad Imp. Manuelem mis*sus* legati munere fungerer et quendam filium meum Hugolinum nomine quem mecum duxeram in itinere morbo correptum amiserim pro redemptione ejus animæ statui vertere è greco in latinum Chrys. expl*anationem* in Joh*annem*'. Nota eundem transtulisse 'prius' Chrys. in Matthæum et Eugenio tertio papæ inscripsisse.

Ejusdem homilia quod nemo leditur nisi a se ipso | idem de reparatione lapsi | idem de compunctione cordis libris duobus | idem in psalmum 50mum 'Miserere mei' et cæt. homilia prima | secunda mutila est.

Codex est lacer et male habitus a plagiariis.   fol.
(*F. 142, s. xiii^2*)

2 Hieronymus in Isaiam codex vetus et bonus sed in quo libri undecim priores excissi sunt per plagiarios et 12mi pars aliqua, cujus finis 'Cum utrum*que* pro diversitate meritorum unus Deus idem*que* condiderit'. Initium 13mi 'Multi casus opprimunt navigantes' et cæt. postrema verba ultimi libri sunt 'Moderatam arbitramur et mixtam clementiæ sententiam judicis'.   fol.
(*F. 82, s. xii med.*)

3* Hieronymus in 12 prophetas minores fol. bon. Nota in initio hujus libri ut ex indiculo in dorso patet, fuisse 'olim' preceptum gloriosi regis Anglorum de possessione et libertate Radingensis monasterii.   fol. bon.
(*B.M., Royal 4 C. ii, s. xii*)

4   Hieronymus in psalmos. In initio desiderantur pauca folia.   fol. bon.
(*F. 81, s. xii*[1])

5* Idem in psalmos quosdam. Primus est 'Dixit Dominus domino meo' et cæt.
Liber vetus literis saxonicis.   4to bon.
(*B.M., Royal 4 A. xiv, s. x*)

6   Idem in canonicas epist*olas* ad modu*m* glossæ.   4to bon.
(*B.M., Royal 2 D. xxvi, s. xiii in.*)

7* Postillæ Nicolai de Lyra in vetus Test. usq*ue* ad finem libri Esther.   fol. rec.
(*F. 25, s. xiv ex.*)

8   Postillæ ejusdem in novum Test.   fol. *eadem manu*
(*F. 28, s. xiv ex.*)

9   Postillæ ejusdem in prophetas ex dono Fr. Joh. Grene anno d*o*mini 1386.
                                                                      fol. *eadem manu*
(*F. 27, s. xiv ex.*)

10 Postillæ ejusdem in psal. prov. eccles. cant. Tob. Jud. Macch. Sapient.
ecclesiasticum et 2m Esdræ.   fol. *eadem manu*
(*F. 26, s. xiv ex.*)

11 Glossa in genesim ex Hier*onymo* Aug*ustino* Gregorio.   fol. *litle* vetus
(*F. 76, s. xii*)

12 Exodus cum glossa ex Aug. Orig. et aliis Patribus.   fol. litle

13* Ruth cum glossa ex Aug. et Orig. et aliis.   4to bon.

14 Greg*orii* moralia in Jobum.   fol. rec.
(*F. 55, s. xiii ex.*)

p. 23, col. 2

15 Aug. de trinitate et super genesin ad literam, ex dono Joh. de Prestone
de Sommersett monachi anno 1348.   fol. rec.
(*F. 11, s. xiv*[1])

16 Aug. de civitate Dei.   fol. rec.
(*This or 17 sent to Westminster, No. 1*)

17 Idem rursus.   fol. rec.
(*This or 16 sent to Westminster, No. 1*)

18* Aug. de verbis d*o*mini secundum Matth. Lucam et Joh. et de verbis
Apostoli. 'Christi (*sic*) tui calicis prædo sit pr*e*da salutis Ære brevi reicis qui
tulit æra crucis'.   fol.
(? *B.M., Royal 5 C. ii, s. xiii*)

19 Aug. de verbis d*o*mini sermones 88 item sermo de verbis apostoli 'Videte
quomodo caute ambuletis' etc.   fol. bon.
(*Sent to Westminster, No. 2*)

20 Aug. confessiones vetus et bonus codex.   fol. litle

21 Idem de libero arbitrio | de gratia et libero arbitrio | de perfectione
justitiæ | de natura et gratia | de correptione et gratia | de prædestinatione
Sanctorum | de bono perseverantiæ | de natura boni | de vera religione | de
doctrina Christiana | de pænitentia | de bono virginitatis | de ecclesiasticis

---

13 *MS.* videtur *interlined beneath* Aug.   20 *A cross against this entry in MS.*

dogmatibus | de 83 questionibus | quæst*iones* 66 | ad Dultitium epistola | de nuptiis et concupiscentiis. 4to recens

22* Aug. de mendacio | de natura et origine animæ libris 2bus | Sermo Arrianorum et Aug. contra eorum perfidiam | 'idem' contra adversarium legis et prophetarum | idem ad Paulinum Nolensem ep*iscopu*m de cura pro mortuis agenda. Initium 'Diu sanctitati tuæ coep*iscop*e venerande Pauline rescriptorum debitor fui' et cæt. | de visitatione infirmorum. Initium est 'Visitationis gratia nepoti meo charissimo morienti extremum valedicturus hesterna die processi' et cæt. |

Sequitur alius tractatus de fide et adventu Christi ut videtur contra Judæos ubi multa de illa prophetia 'Non auferetur *sceptrum* de *tribu Judæ*'. Initium est 'Magna dissensio est inter filios hominum cum de multis aliis tum de fidei confessione' et cæt. Finis 'sed est potius sententia data à do*mi*no quod perpetua sit hęc desolatio vestra quod in loco suo satis demonstrabitur, quæ vobis jam circiter annos mille persolvit, nihil fraudaturus vobis de cæteris us*que* in fine*m*' |

Sequitur alius tract. 'Usu pariter et necessitate didicimus vel ad amicos ut consulant vel ad medicos ut curent confugere vulneratos.' Epistola est forte Fulberti cujus quędam infra sequuntur | postea alius tractatus. Initium 'Patres venerab. charissimi filii dei aliquid vobis volumus memorare de his quę vos nunquam oblivisci oportet' | Fulbertus Carnot*ensis* ep*iscopu*s ad Litericum Senon*ensis* archiep*iscopu*m, 'De pres*by*te*r*o vestro' | ejusdem alia ad R. *Sancti* Medardi abbatem, 'Quum (*sic*) diu de vobis' | ejusdem G. abbati, 'Præsul Aurelianorum qui vos excommunicavit' | et aliæ Fulberti epistolę et Roberti regis Galliarum de pluvia sanguinis in Aquitania ad Guazlinum et alios et [cæt.].

(*B.M., Royal 5 A. xiii, s. xii*) 4to bon. vetus

p. 24, col. 1

23* Aug. contra quin*que* hæreses | symbolum Nicænum et aliæ confessiones fidei ut Greg. Nyss. | de naturis quorundam animaliu*m* videtur Epiphanii, 'Physiologus leone' est initium | Disputatio regalis Pippini juvenis et Alcuini. Initium 'Quid est litera? R. Custos historiæ. quid est verbum? proditor animi' et cæt. 8vo vet.

24 Aug. in apoc*alypsin* jussu Dunstani abbatis script. literis saxonicis. 4to bon. (*Bodleian, Hatton 30, s. x*)

25 Aug. retract*ationes* | de utilitate credendi | de gratia novi Test. | de qualitate vis*ionis* beatorum ex ultimo libro de civitate Dei. 4to (*B.M., Royal 5 A. xiv, s. xii*)

26 Registrum B. Greg*orii*. fol. bon. (*B.M., Royal 6 C. vii, s. xii*)

27 Sermones varii Aug., Bedæ, Leonis, Faustini et Gregorii. fol. bon. (*F. 93, s. xii*[1])

28* Epistolæ Hieronymi. Nota unam esse ad Tranquillinum de lectione Origenis. fol. bon. (? *B.M., Royal 6 D. iii, s. xii*)

---

22 *A star against the entry* 'De visitatione infirmorum' *in MS.*

29* Aug. de verbis domini | de baptismo parvulorum | de patientia | Anselmus de beatitudine cælestis patriæ | Dionysius de ierarchia angelorum 'et ecclesiastica et divinis nominibus et epistolę' translatus a Joh. Sarraceno et inscriptus Joh. de Sarisburiis | de fide et legibus secundum Parisiensem, 'In ordine sapientialium' et cæt. | de virtutibus idem, 'Postquam jam claruit ex ordine ipso rerum divinalium' et cæt. | Aug. de sermone domini in monte | confessiones ejusdem | Richardus de Sancto Victore de trinitate.   fol. rec.
(F. 32, s. xiii)

30 Aug. de trinitate | Richardus de Sancto Victore de eadem | sermo Aug. de oratione et jejunio | idem de ecclesiasticis dogmatibus | et de libero arbitrio et gratia.   fol. rec.
(F. 149, s. xiii²)

31* Tabula super Aug. ordine alphabeti | item super librum moralium Gregorii et temporale homiliarum Magistri Odonis.   4to recens
(Q. 24, s. xiii/xiv)

32 Anselmus de similitudinibus | de meditationibus | orationes ad Sanctos | prosologion et cæt. [see page 59].   fol.
(F. 132, s. xiv)

33 Anselmi varia et Bernardus de dispensatione et præcepto, in fine sunt paucæ epistolę ejusdem [see page 59].   fol.
(Sent to Westminster, No. 3)

34* Anselmi rursus varia ubi et quædam epistolæ habentur [see page 60].   fol.
(F. 41, s. xiv in.)

35 Isidori Hispalensis quæstiones. Initium 'Inter deum et dominum ita quidam definierunt' | Fulberti quædam epistolæ ad Deodatum quę opusculo præfigitur (sic) cujus initium 'Tria siquidem nobis sunt ad perfectum christianæ religionis proposita' et cæt. | ejusdem epist. ad Finardum (sic) de hostia | Ivonis duæ epistolæ, Galoni et Hildeberto | de tabernaculo domini anonym., 'Faciant mihi sanctuarium filii Israel' et cæt. | Sequitur alius tract. sine titulo videtur Isidori, 'Principium et caussa omnium Deus ante omnia æternaliter' et cæt. | Anselmus de processione spiritus Sancti | Floccelli martyris sub Antonio et Maximiano passio.   8vo
(B.M., Royal 5 E. v, s. xii)

p. 24, col. 2

36 Vita Gregorii papæ per Johannem.   fol.
(B.M., Royal 6 A. vii, s. xi in.)

37* Pastorale Gregorii.   4to
(This or 38 is ? Glasgow, Hunterian V. 5. 1, s. x–xii, or sent to Westminster, No. 4)

38 Rursus.   4to bon.
(This or 37 is ? Glasgow, Hunterian V. 5. 1 or sent to Westminster, No. 4)

39 Rursus una cum sermonibus cujusdam anonymi primus est in illa verba

---

35 MS. 4to written first, then scratched out and 8vo substituted.

'Arcta est via quæ ducit ad vitam. Mirabile est in oculis meis quod sanctitati vestræ ac discretioni debeo loqui qui non sum doctus nec legis peritus'.   4to
(*B.M., Royal 5 E. xii, s. xiii*)

40   Homiliæ Greg*orii* de diversis lectionibus evang*elii*. bonus et vetus.   fol. litle
(*Q. 21, s. x*)

41* Fulgentius de fide Donato | Aug. de utilitate agendæ pœnit*entiæ* | idem de disciplina christiana | de decem chordis | idem ad Valerium Comitem, 'O mi frater si cupias' et cæt. desideratur finis item epistola Wintoniensis ad Alexandrum Pontificem et Alexandri ad Lanfrancum prout ex indiculo veteri qui in dorso libri est videre licet et vestigiis plagii | in fine est Aug. de ecclesiasticis dogmatibus.   fol. bon.
(*B.M., Royal 5 B. iii, s. xii*)

42   Leonis papæ epistolæ 71 postrema est ad Torvulum (*sic*) ep*iscopum* Austuriensem, prima autem ad Eutycen p*res*b*yter*um Constantinopolitanum.   fol. bon.
(*Q. 7, s. xii²*)

43* Bernardus de consideratione | de amore Dei | epist*ola* ad Hugonem | alia ad Petrum abelardum | 'item ad Innocentium alia' | idem super Missus est sive de laudibus B. Virginis | idem de discreta varietate ordinis monastici | idem contra Cisterciensium detractiones | et contra superfluitates Cluniacensium | idem de gradibus humilitatis | Jeremias cum glossa | admonitio ad claustrales, 'De ordine fratrum claustralium loquuturi et pauca dicturi'. fol.
(*Q. 51, s. xii²–xiii in.*)

44   Bernardus de laudibus Virg*inis* | Aug. de vera charitate | Aug. de decem præceptis et plagis | Bernard*us* de amore Dei | idem de diligendo Deo | Innocentius de contemptu mundi | Seneca de verborum copia, 'Quisquis prudentiam sequi desideras' et cæt. | ejusdem proverbia ordine alphabeti | de cessatione legalium Lincolni*ensis* | Bernard*us* de præcepto et dispensatione | idem de discreta varietate ordinis monastici | de gradibus humilitatis | idem ad Eugenium de consideratione.   fol. recens
(*F. 152, s. xiv ex.*)

45   Hugo in Lamentationes | Bernardi sermo, 'Circumire possum d*omi*ne cælum et terram' et cæt. | Lundinensis ecclesiæ minister anonymus in orat*ionem* dominicam, opusculum inscribitur Waltero Hereford. archidiacono, 'Sacra vestræ petitionis me compellit instantia' | de 12 abusionibus, 'Sunt quidam qui sciunt et possunt præesse' et cæt. | de claustro animæ, 'Nosti charissime quod ea quæ de ordinatione claustri materialis diximus' et cæt. Vide an Hugonis sint duo posteriores tract.   4to
(*Q. 48, s. xii ex.*)

p. 25, col. 1
46   Joh. Damascenus de fide orthodoxa.   4to rec.
(*Q. 76, s. xiv in.*)

---

41 *A star against this entry in MS.*   42 *A star against this entry in MS.*
43 *In MS. the words* super Missus est *are lined through.*
44 *A cross against the Grosseteste item in MS. The words* scala humilitatis et scala superbiæ *are lined through in MS. after* humilitatis.
45 *A star against this entry in MS.*

47* Beda in Marcum, 'Omnis scriba doctus in regno cælorum' et cæt. fol. bon.
(*F. 83, s. xii*[2])

48   Manipulus florum sive tabula originalium ex 36 auctoribus per Thomam
de Hybernia quondam socium de Serbona et Joh. Galensem ordinis fra*trum*
minorum, ordine alphabeti.   fol. rec.
(*F. 153, s. xiv*)

49   Excerpta ex 23 auctoribus Patribus et aliis.   fol. rec.
(*F. 51, s. xiv in.*)

50* Damascenus de fide orthodoxa ex tralatione Burgundionis judicis Pisani |
item Dionysii areopagitæ opera omnia lat*ine* per eundem | Aug. de 12 abusivis |
Bedæ versus de die judicii | Aug. retractationes | idem de hæresibus | vita Aug.
per Possidium | sermo Aug. de ora*tione* dominica | ejusdem de incarna*tione*
filii sermo | de doctrina christiana | enchiridion | de bono mortis | de inmortali-
tate animæ | de sancta virginitate | quæstiones Orosii | de ecclesiasticis dogma-
tibus et definitionibus rectæ fidei | de duabus animabus | Aug. de magistro
dialogisticœs | de potentia et ejus objecto incerti, 'Potentia quædam habet
objectum' et cæt. | expositio magistralis in cantici quædam, 'Quasi cedrus
exaltata sum in Libano' et cæt. Initium 'Multiplices proprietates sunt ar-
borum' |
Aug. de vera innocentia | de disciplina Christianorum | de imagine | de
mirabilibus novi et vet. test. | de bono conjugali | de bono viduitatis | de
symbolo serm*ones* 4or | de timore d*omini* | de videndo Deo | contra 5 hæreses |
de mendacio et contra mendacium | de fide et operibus | de vera religione | unde
malum | de libero arbitrio | Soliloquia | epistola ad Donatum | de fide S*anctæ*
trinitatis | Isidorus de ordine creaturarum, 'Universitatis dispositio bifaria
ratione debet intelligi'. Nota Anselmi quasdam episto*las* fuisse in hoc codice
olim sed jam ablatas.   fol.
(*F. 57, s. xiii*)

51* Bernardi flores | Bernardi quædam verba melliflua | Comment. in Joelem
proph. | Postillæ in Exodum Hug*onis* de Brisingham, 'O filia principis cant. 8.
Divinæ sapientiæ summa et incomprehensibilis et inscrutabilis prudentia'
et cæt.   fol.
(*F. 84, s. xiii*)

52   Bernardus de lamentatione M. Virg. | Anselmi meditatio ad excitandam
devotionem | Bernardi meditationes | et cæt. vide et adde sermo Joh. eleemo-
synarii ad humilitatis exemplum | Regula Basilii | Vita Francisci | Cæsarii
homiliæ ad monachos | sermo Aug. de mundi gloria et aliis | idem de decem
chordis | et de conflictu virtutum et vitiorum | Hieronymi ad Heliodorum
'et alios epistolæ aliquot' | Hugo de arrha animæ | de claustro animæ liber,
'Diversorum ædificiorum diversa est ratio' | Anselmi meditatio de redemptione
humani generis | epistola Hieronymi ad Demetriadem et cæt.   fol. litle
(*F. 75, s. xiii*[2])

---

50 diversis *scored through before* hæresibus *in MS.*
51 *Young first wrote* Bernardi flores et cæt. fol. *Later he cancelled* et cæt. fol. *and added
the rest in a small hand.*   *MS.* princicipis.

p. 25, col. 2

53 Lanfrancus de corpore et sanguine domini contra Berengarium, opus est dialogisticum, 'Si divina pietas cordi tuo inspirare dignaretur' et cæt. | Berengarii confessio fidei, 'Quotiens deum cogitare volumus minus utique volumus quam debeamus' et cæt. | Rhabanus de corpore et sanguine domini, 'Quisquis catholicorum' et cæt. | Ambrosius de pænitentia libris 2bus.   4to bon.
(*B.M., Royal 5 F. xii, s. xii*)

54 Admonitiones simplices parrochiis necessariæ; ubi primum est Athanasii symbolum | deinde de fratrum concordia homilia. de væ pregnantibus et nutrientibus. de calendis Januarii. de auguriis. de castitatis bono contra concubinarum usum. de diligendis inimicis. de vera charitate. de ebrietate. rursus de eadem. de castitate servanda et de uxoribus. de indigna familiaritate. de martyribus. de illo 'Venite benedicti'. de reddendis decimis. de parochiis. de templo. charactere saxonico.   4to

55* Biblia latina.   4to
(*Bodleian, Auct. D. inf. 2. 4, s. xiii*)

56 Comment. in psalmos anonym. Initium 'Cum istud tam dignissimum opus totum in prophetia contineatur' et cæt. in fine desiderantur quædam. fol.

57 Psalterium et pars missalis.   4to bon.
(? *F. 160, s. xiii*[1])

58 Prophetæ 12 cum glossa vet*us*.   4to bon.
(*Q. 8, s. xii*[2])

59 Jeremias et Daniel cum glossa.   4to
(*B.M., Royal 3 A. viii, s. xiii*)

60 Prophetæ 12 cum glossa.   fol.
(*Sent to Westminster, No. 5*)

61 Expositio sive glossa in 12 proph. et Job.   fol.
(*B.M., Royal 2 E. xi, s. xiii ex.*)

62 Distinctiones Cestrensis monachi, 'Abjicere. Secundum physiologos columba propter calorem quem habet abjicit feces de nido suo et idem docet pullos suos facere' et cæt. Holcot in librum Sapientiæ. Initium 'Dominus petra [mea] et robur meum' et cæt. imperf.   fol. rec.
(*F. 128, s. xiv ex.*)

63 In ecclesiasticum forte idem Holcot. Initium est 'Sapientia ædificavit sibi domum' et cæt.   fol. rec.
(*F. 52, s. xiii*[2])

64 Postilla in Matthæum, ac primum in prologum. In*itium* 'Præsens prologus in tres partes dividitur'.   fol. rec.
(*F. 67, s. xiv in.*)

65 Marcus cum glossa | expositio Richardi (abbatis Pratellensis) in canticum Canticorum, opus inscribitur Mauricio cuidam quem filium vocat. Initium

---

62 Distinctiones Cestrensis monachi *written over* Holcot in librum Sapientiæ, *which has been cancelled.*

'Salomon tres libros qui in canone sacrę scripturæ recipiuntur composuit' et cæt. Desiderantur quædam in fine. 4to bon.
(*Q. 16, s. xii med.–xiii*[1])

66 Lucas cum glossa ve*tus*. 4to
(*Q. 82, s. xii*)

67 Pauli epistolæ cum glossa | tractatus theologicus distinctus in capita 196 nisi quædam in fine desint. Initium 'Quoniam homo peccando tam voluntate quam opere suum offendit conditorem' et cæt. fol. bon.
(*B.M., Royal 2 F. 1, s. xiii in.*)

p. 26, col. 1

68* Evangelium Joh. cum glossa. fol. l*itle*
(*Q. 94, s. xii ex.–xiii in.*)

69 Glossæ in epistolas Pauli imperf. fol. l*itle*
(*F. 49, s. xii*)

70 Bedæ expositio in Marcum | in fine est dialogus inter animam et corpus 'prosa et carmine' imitatio est Boetii. Initium 'Incendio domus mea corruerat et reficiendi studio sollicitus inhiabam'. fol. bon.
(*B.M., Royal 4 B. xiii, s. xii ex.*)

71 Josephus de bello Judaico et antiquit. fol. rec.
(*F. 9, s. xiii ex.*)

72* Rabanus de naturis rerum imperf. fol. bon.
(*F. 21, s. xiii in.*)

73 Ambrosii epistolæ | ad finem est tractatus de morte Theodosii ejusdem | sequitur tractatus de Sanctis Gervasio et Protasio inventis et depositis. Init. 'Quia nihil sanctitatem tuam soleo eorum præterire quæ hic te absente gerantur' et cæt. | sequitur item historia Nabuthæ. Initium 'Nabuthæ historia tempore vetus est usu quotidiano' et cæt. in fine quædam desiderantur. vet*us*. fol. litle
(? *B.M., Royal 6 A. xvi, s. xii*)

74 Postills in english, papier. 8vo

75 Missale mutilum in initio secundum usum Sarum procul dubio. 8vo
(*Q. 10, s. xv*)

76 Bernardi sermones in illud, 'Missus est Angelus Gabriel' | lucerna conscientiæ. Initium 'Si diligitis me mandata mea servate. Cogitanti mihi sedenti solitario quid faciendo' et cæt. | speculum humanæ salvationis 'rithmice' dividitur in capitula 85qu*e* | Hugo de quinqu*e* septenis | Aug. ad Julianu*m* comitem | Hieronym*us* de induratione cordis Pharaonis | Hieronym*us* ad Eustochium | et Asellam | speculum spiritualis amicitiæ Aluredi | Summa de confessione Thomæ Wallensis | Hieron*ymus* ad Demetriadem | Aug. de doctrina Christiana | commoniloquium Tho. (*sic*) Wallensis. fol. rec.
(*F. 114, s. xv*)

77* Narratio de inventione Sanctæ crucis | homiliæ Aug. | Bedæ | Rabani | Leonis in festivitates sanctorum | ubi et Ambrosii Gregorii et Alcuini sunt quidam et Fulberti de nativitate Sanctæ Mariæ, 'Approbatæ consuetudinis est apud

---

77 *The words* et Fulberti . . . et cæt. *are added in margin and between the lines.*

Christianos *Sanctorum* patrum dies natalitios observare diligenter' et cæt. |
item Anselmus de excellentia B. Vir*ginis*. fol. bon.
(*F. 94, s. xii*[1])

78* Postillæ in epistolas Pauli ex Aug. Chrysost*omo* Ambr*osio* et Greg*orio*. fol.
(*F. 143, s. xiii*)

79 Psalterium cum glossa. fol.
(*Sent to Westminster, No. 6*)

80* Petri Trecensis ad Gul. Senonensem epi*scopu*m historia ecclesiastica imperf. |
Exodus cum glossa | Vitæ beatorum patrum per Hiero*nymum* imperfect. Initium
'præf.' 'Benedictus deus qui vult omnes homines salvos fieri' et cæt. | Homiliæ
40 Gregorii papæ super evangelia | Origenis homilia in illud 'Cum esset despon-
sata mater Jesu Maria' et cæt. | Bedæ homilia in illud 'In principio erat verbum'
et cæt. | item alia in illud 'Pastores loquebantur ad invicem' et cæt. | Bernardus
super 'Missus est angelus' | Homiliæ dominicales æstivales anonym*ωs* | distinc-
tiones theologicæ anon. | tractatus M*agist*ri Richardi super illud 'Qui bene
præsunt' et cæt. | exempla quædam ex legenda hausta | tractatus in epistolas
Pauli. fol.
(*F. 71, s. xii–xiii*)

81 Glossa in epistolas Pauli imperf. fol.
(*Sent to Westminster, No. 7*)

82 Figuræ cum moralitate de Genesi us*que* ad finem apocalypsis anon. fol. rec.
(*Q. 93, s. xv in.*)

p. 26, col. 2

83 Magister historiarum sive scolastica historia ab initio Joh. Hircani us*que*
ad finem actuum apostolorum. 4to
(*Q. 2, s. xiii in.*)

84 Distinctiones Januensis | Redewaus in Ovidii metamorphosim. fol. rec.
(*F. 89, s. xiv ex.*)

85 Robertus Holcot in librum sapientiæ. fol.
(*F. 155, s. xiv/xv*)

86 Psalmi cum glossa. fol.
(*F. 47, s. xiii*[1])

87 Festivitatum domini expositiones et congruar*um* lectionum ex evang*eliis*
et epist*olis* Pauli | ubi etiam quædam expos*itiones* lectionum martyrum et
virginum habentur. vetus. fol. bon.
(*F. 91, s. xi*[1])

88 Historia scholastica Petri Trecensis. fol.
(*F. 33, s. xiii, or F. 37: cf. nos. 91, 93*)

89 Eusebii ecclesiastica hist*oria* vet*us*. 4to bon.
(*Q. 28, s. x*)

90 Glossa in decreta 'Fr. de Bromesgrave' | et historiæ scolasticæ pars. 4to
(*Q. 44, s. xii ex.–xii/xiii*)

---

80 *A star against the last line of this entry in MS.*

91   Historia schola*stica*.   fol.
(*This or 93 is F. 37, or F. 33 (cf. no. 88), or sent to Westminster, No. 8*)

92   Historia scholastica | tractatus quidam anon. de grammatica 'vel potius
rhetorica'. Initium, 'Ferrum situ rubiginem ducit et vitis non amputata in
labruscam silvescit' | nota post figurarum troporum et similium definitiones
percurrere authorem libros *sanctæ* scripturę omnes et inde exempla petere.   4to
(*F. 1, s. xiii*)

93   Historia scholastica.   fol.
(*This or 91 is F. 37, s. xiii/xiv, or F. 33 (cf. no. 88), or sent to Westminster, No. 8*)

94   Vocabularius Bibliæ.   fol. rec.
(*F. 130, s. xiv*)

95   Vocabularius alter nominum hæb*raicorum* et latinorum.   fol. litle
(*F. 34, s. xiii²*)

96*   Expositiones vocabulorum vet. et novi test. anon. deest finis 'ordine
librorum servato'. Initium est 'Cum animadverterem frater R. charissime
quosdam novitios nimium circa vocabula quæ ignorant negligentes' et cæt. |
Brito de eisdem 'ordine alph*abeti*' | summula Cantoris Paris*iensis* de tropicis
locutionibus, 'Videmus nunc per speculum et in ænigmate' et cæt. | Cassiodorus
de figuris et tropis locutionum, 'Solet aliquotiens in scripturis ordo verborum
causa decoris' | Gull*iel*mus de Monte de tropis, 'Dei dona dispensamus pul-
santibus' et cæt. | Grammatica R. Hambury nobilis magistri, 'Effectum gram-
maticæ quærere sitientes primitus oportet noscere quid sit grammatica'. fol. rec.
(*F. 61, s. xiv*)

97   Homiliæ et sermones ab adventu d*om*ini ad pascha ex diversis Chrys*ostomo*
Beda Augu*stino* Orig*ene* Hieron*ymo* Leone et Greg*orio*.   fol. bon.
(*F. 92, s. xii¹*)

98*   Expositiones ex diversis patribus in evang*eliorum* et epistol*arum* lectiones,
præf. initium 'Cernens in ecclesia plurimos divinarum scripturarum mysticos
nugaciter perquirere sensus' et cæt. ex Hil*ario* Hieron*ymo* Augu*stino* Cyprian*o*
Cyrill*o* Greg*orio* Fulgent*io* Cassiod*oro* Beda et aliis anonymus.   fol. bon.
(*Bodleian, Barlow 4, s. xi in.*)

99*   Sermones M*agistr*i Joh. Lawren | sermo in visitatione, 'Fratres tuos
visitabis' et cæt. | in synodo | in dedicatione eccl*es*iæ | in consecratione virg*inis* |
in professione | de assumpt*ione* B. Virg*inis* | et cæt. anonym. | Item Bonifacii
papę liber ad Oxon.   fol. rec.
(*F. 126, s. xiv/xv*)

p. 27, col. 1

100   Sermones Fra*tris* Guiberti de Thornaco. Initium 'Exequutis inspirante
domino sex partibus tractatus cujus est titulus de conditione doctoris restat
pars septima quam habemus in manibus difficilior et diffusior de doctrina
sc*ilicet* hominis pertinente ad prædicatores seu experimentum practicæ' | in-
scriptum est opus Alexandro quarto pontifici.   fol. rec.
(*F. 36, s. xiii/xiv*)

---

96 verborum *altered to* vocabulorum.   *Young notes in the margin* Prometheus Huberti
monachi.

101   Sermones Fr*atris* Draconis tribus libris.   fol. rec.
(*F. 5, s. xiv*[1])

102* Summa Joh. de Rupella de decem præceptis | tractatus de 'quatuor'
virt*utibus* card*inalibus* et 7tem vitiis capitalibus. | Aug. homilia de decem plagis
et de decem præceptis | tractatus de pænitentia confessione et cæt. | de officio
missæ miracula quædam B. Virg*inis*.   litle fol. rec.

103   Vocabularius Bibliæ, 'Cum animadverterem fr. R. charissime quosdam
novitios'. author est Hubertus monachus libri nomen Prometheus. litle fol. rec.
(*Sent to Westminster, No. 9*)

104   Magister sententiarum.   fol.
(*The eight copies listed by Young, nos. 104, 128–33, 147, are represented apparently
by the present F. 8 (s. xiii), 46 (s. xiii), 53 (s. xiii*[2]*), 88 (s. xiii), 98 (s. xiii), 134
(s. xiii ex.), Q. 47 (s. xiii) and the MS sent to Westminster, No. 11*)

105   Sermones Guiberti de Tornaco 'ordinis Fr*atrum* min*orum*', idem est qui
supra.   fol. litle
(*F. 77, s. xiv*)

106   Lectura Kilwarby in libros sententiarum. Initium 'Sapientia ædificavit
sibi domum excidit columnas. in his verbis attendi possunt quatuor'.   fol.
(*F. 43, s. xiii ex.*)

107* Sermones Meldenham. Initium 'Spiritus passus est vobis relinquens
exemplum ut sequamini'. sermo est de passione Christi.   fol. rec.
(*F. 10, s. xv*)

108   Sermones Repingtoni. Initium 'Evangelicæ tubæ comminatio' et cæt.
                                                                    fol. rec.
(*F. 121, s. xv*)

109   Sermones de tempore et sanctis anonymi. Initium 'Lætabor ego super
eloquia tua'. 'de valle scholarium'.   fol. rec.
(*F. 16, s. xiii/xiv*)

110   Sermones Jacobi de Losanna 'de tem*pore* et sanctis', 'Sicut in die honeste
ambulemus' et cæt.   4to
(*Sent to Westminster, No. 10*)

111* Sermones nonnulli de diversis festis.   4to
(*Q. 11, s. xiii in.*)

112* Temporale sive sermones de tempore, 'Emitte manum tuam' et cæt.
Vide an sit Blesensis, ut est in catalogo Paulinæ bibliothecæ pag. 3.   4to rec.
(*Q. 65, s. xiv*)

113   Sermones varii, 'Qui sunt isti qui ut nubes volant'.   4to imperf.
(*Q. 6, s. xiii in.–xiii*[1])

114* Postillæ Gul. Bedmyster. 'Penuria studentium in...morali pauper-
tas*que* juvenum qui copia privantur librorum', compilat*e* ex operibus Januensis,
Paris*iensis*, Lugd*unensis*, Odonis et aliorum.   4to rec.
(*Q. 45, s. xv*)

102, 103 *MS.* 4to *altered to* litle fol. *in each entry.*
112 *The words* Vide an...pag. 3 *are in the margin.*
114 *Young could not read the word between* in *and* morali: *it should be* 'materia'.

115   De Virgine Maria Joh. Stamuch (*sic*) Carmelita, 'Hoc nomen Maria habet 5 literas' et cæt. | tractatus de volucribus et bestiis et earum naturis cum applicatione, 'Duæ sunt species accipitris' et cæt. | sermones varii.   4to
(*Q.56, s. xv*)

p. 27, col. 2

116   Historia scholastica Petri Trecensis dicti Comestoris, in fine est ejus epitaphium

> Petrus eram quem petra tegit dictus*que* comestor
> Nunc comedor, vivus docui nec cesso docere
> Mortuus ut dicat qui me videt incineratum
> Quod sumus iste fuit, erimus quandoq*ue* quod hic est.   fol.

(*F. 133, s. xiii*)

117   Sermones varii imperf., 'Veni de libano'.   8vo
(*Q.77, s. xiii*)

118   Logica et philosophia Joh. Dumbleton novem lib*ris*, 'Plurimorum scribentium'.   fol.
(*F. 6, s. xiv/xv*)

119   Sermones varii anonymi, 'Benedictionem dabit legislator'.   4to litle

120   Liber sermonum de sanctis initium a Sa*n*cto Laurentio, 'Igne me examinasti'.   4to rec.
(*Q.9, s. xiv in.*)

121   Sermones Guidonis Fr. de ordine prædicatorum quos in conventu Ebroicensi compilavit, 'Nunc enim proprior (*sic*) est nostra salus'.   8vo
(*Q.12, s. xiv*)

122   Postillæ anonymi. Initium 'Festivitates Sa*n*ctorum apostolorum seu martyrum antiqui patres in venerationis ministerio celebrari sanxerunt' | quinq*ue* libri Mosis. Initium præfationis translatoris quisquis fuerit, 'Frater Ambrosius mihi tua munuscula perferens detulit suavissimas literas' et cæt. | est et alia pręfixa tran*s*lationi epistola ad Desiderium, Initium est 'Desiderii mei desideratas accepi literas' et cæt. in qua de 70 interpretum versione græca et Origenis octoplo et Theodotionis versione.   4to
(*Q.61, s. xiii[1]*)

123* Sermones anon. | sermones item Richardi de Theford, 'Ductus est Jesus in desertum' | tractatus de irregularitatibus indigentibus dispensationem apostolicam.   4to
(*Q.67, s. xiii[1]*)

124   Tractatus quidam grammatici | primi initium 'Qui bene vult disponere familiæ suæ vel domui vel rebus suis primo provideat sibi in utensilibus et in supellectilibus' et cæt. | 2i 'Cum ad cujuslibet scientiæ clericalis cognitione*m* necessarium sit grammaticæ fundamentum' | 3i præfat. initium 'Quoniam ignorantiæ nubilo turpiter excæcati': tractatus ipse est carmine scriptus. Initium 'Est proprie metha trans gręce formatio plasma' et cæt.   4to
(*Q.50, s. xiii*)

---

115 moralitate *is written above* applicatione.   122 octoplo *underlined.*

125 Sermones Jacobi de Losanna et aliorum. 8vo
(*Q. 19, s. xiii ex.*)

126 Interprętationes nominum hæbreorum *sanctæ* scripturæ | Eucherius de
locis sanctis Fausto *presbytero* insulano. Initium 'Hierosolymitanæ urbis situm'
et cæt. | Hieronymi epistola ad Dardanum de terra repromissionis | Aug. de
immor*talitate* animæ | de spiritu et anima | soliloquia | de quantitate animæ |
epistola ad Paulinam | expositio in librum sapientiæ initium deest [p. 28, col. 1]
finis est, 'ad illam magnitudinem nos perducat Jesus Christus d*ominus* noster
qui et benedictus in secula seculorum Amen' | in canticum Canticorum. Initium
'Cantabo dilecto meo canticum triplex' | et in apocalypsin, initium 'Eleganter
ordinavit divinæ sapientiæ providentia' | de pænitentia tractatus, initium
'Misericors et miserator d*ominus*'. fol.
(*F. 124, s. xiii–xiv*)

127 Ludolphus de vita Christi. fol. rec.
(*F. 140, s. xv*)

128 Magister sententiarum. fol.
(*For Nos. 128–33, see No. 104*)

129 Rursus idem. fol.

130 Rursus idem. fol.

131 Rursus idem. fol.

132 Rursus idem. fol.

133 Rursus idem. fol. litle

134 Liber q*uartus* sententiarum 'et S*anctus* Thomas in eundem' | et distinc-
tiones quædam. Initium 'Deus canticum novum cantabo tibi' et cæt. 4to
(*Q. 88, s. xiii*)

135 Anonymus quidam in senten*tias* per compendium. 4to
(*Q. 35, s. xiii²*)

136 Thomas in primum sentent*iarum*. fol.
(*F. 107, s. xiv in.*)

137* Sequax magistri. Initium 'Invisibilia Dei a creatura mundi per ea quæ
facta sunt, intellecta perspiciuntur' | forte Hugonis de tribus diebus tractatus
cujus idem est initium. fol.
(*F. 54, s. xiii¹*)

138 Thomas in 3m sentent*iarum*. fol.
(*F. 108, s. xiv*)

139 Thomas in 4tum sent*entiarum*. fol.
(*F. 109, s. xiii/xiv*)

140 Thomas in primam 2æ | item tertia pars summæ ejusdem. fol.
(*F. 104, s. xiii/xiv*)

141 Idem in 2am 2æ. fol.
(*F. 102, s. xiii ex.*)

---

126 *Three stars against the latter part of this entry.*
137 *The words* forte…initium *are in the margin and are instead of the words* puto esse
Pulli. confer cum codice bibliothecæ regiæ, *which have been cancelled. A star in the
margin against the entry.*

142 Rursus in primam 2æ.   fol.
(*F. 101, s. xiv in.*)

143 Rursus in 2am 2æ.   fol.
(*F. 103, s. xiii/xiv*)

144 Thomas de potentia et malo.   fol.
(*F. 105, s. xiv*)

145 Bonaventura in 4tum sent*entiarum*.   fol.
(*F. 167, s. xiii ex.*)

146 Thomas de fide catholica contra gentes.   fol.
(*F. 106, s. xiv*)

147 Magister sententiarum.   fol. litle
(*See note to No. 104*)

148 Bonaventura in 4tum sent*entiarum*.   fol. litle
(*Q. 69, s. xiii/xiv*)

149 Joh. Duns super 4or libros sent*entiarum*.   fol.
(*F. 69, s. xiv in.*)

150 Magister sentent*iarum* imperf.   fol.
(*F. 64, s. xii/xiii*)

151 Quotlibeta M*agist*ri Godefridi de fontibus cancellarii paris*iensis* | lectura
anon. in 3es libros sentent*iarum* | quæstiones Stephani e*pisco*pi paris*iensis* in
sententias | quotlibeta M. Thom*æ* de Alliaco (*sic*).   fol.
(*F. 56, s. xiii²*)

p. 28, col. 2

152 Summa Antisiodorensis.   fol.
(*F. 31, s. xiii²*)

153 Quæstiones in libros sent*entiarum* anon. | et orationis dominicæ ex-
positio.   fol.
(*F. 50, s. xiii*)

154 Sententi*a*rum quartus liber cum glossa.   fol.
(*F. 176, s. xiii med.*)

155 Frater Joh. de Alston (*sic*) in sent*entias*.   4to
(*Q. 33, s. xiii*)

156 Expositio in sent*entias* anon.   4to
(*Q. 20, s. xiii/xiv*)

157 Determinationes 'septem' quotlibetorum Henrici de Gandavo, 'Quere-
bamur (*sic*) in nostra generali disput*atione*'.   fol.
(*F. 79, s. xiii/xiv*)

158 Idem rursus.   fol.
(*Sent to Westminster, No. 12*)

159 Quæstiones in libros sent*entiarum*. Initium 'Fides est substantia rerum
sperandaru*m*'.   fol.
(*F. 44, s. xiii*)

160 Quæstionista quidam de eis quæ pertinent ad personarum distinctionem. Initium 'Pertractatis hucusque de eis quæ in deo ad communem pertinent substantiam'.   fol.
(*F. 164, s. xiv in.*)

161* Quæstiones in 4or libros sententiarum.   fol.
(*F. 139, s. xiv in.*)

162 Quæstiones diversæ theologicæ, 'Ut (*sic*) charitas possit augeri' et cæt.   4to
(*Q. 71, s. xiv*)

163* Quæstionista in sententias.   fol.
(*F. 39, s. xiv*)

164 Quæstiones theologicæ et philosophicæ.   4to
(*Q. 31, s. xiii*)

165 Distinctiones Fr. Mauritii.   4to
(*Q. 42, s. xiii ex.*)

166 Libri novem codicis Justiniani.   fol.
(*F. 78, s. xiii*)

167* Institutiones cum glossa ab initio vocatur liber, 'Prometheus in Caucasi montis cacumine religatus' et cæt.   4to
(*B.M., Harley 4967*)

168 De ordine judiciorum liber. Initium 'Assiduis postulationibus mei socii mei charissimi' et cæt. | cavillationes Bagaroti, 'Precibus et instantia congruenti' et cæt. | Item alius, 'Cum plures libelli super variis caussarum exercitiis | una cum aliis tractatibus in jure civili'.   4to
(*F. 74, s. xiii–xiv*)

169 Liber institutionum | et Brocarda domini Ottonis.   fol.
(*F. 14, s. xiii*[1])

170 Comment. in Justinianum.   fol.
(*F. 24, s. xii*)

171 Digestum novum.   fol.
(*F. 136, s. xiii/xiv*)

172 Idem rursus.   fol.
(*Sent to Westminster, No. 13*)

173 Digestum inforciatum.   fol.
(*F. 135, s. xiii*[2])

174* Decretales.   fol.
(? *F. 110, s. xiii*[2])

175 Decretalium liber sextus 'unde multa excisa'.   fol.
(? *F. 97, s. xiv*[2])

176 Innocentius super decretales.   fol.
(*Sent to Westminster, No. 14*)

---

166 MS. fol. *altered from* 4to.
168 *The words* in fine hujus (?) *are scored out before* cavillationes.

p. 29, col. 1

177 Quinque libri Innocentii super decretales. fol.
(*F. 170, s. xiii ex.*)

178 Speculum juris canonici summa summarum vocatur. fol.
(*F. 131, s. xiv*)

179 Summa de jure canonico. fol.
(*F. 90, s. xiv*)

180 Summa Godfredi super titulis decretalium | summula item Barth.
Brixiensis juris canonici | summa Magistri Laurentii de Sommercot canonico (*sic*)
Cicestrensi 1254to | Item summa Raynfredi de libellis in jure canonico. fol.
(*F. 100, s. xiv in.*)

181 Casus decretalium et decretorum. fol.
(*F. 159, s. xiii¹*)

182* Hugo super decreta. fol.
(*F. 12, s. xiii*)

183* Leges et decreta Gratiani imperf. fol.
(*Cf. Appendix III, no. 1*)

184 Glossa Guidonis super sextum decretalium et apparatus Joh. Andree
in eundem. fol.
(*F. 141, s. xiv*)

185 Monaldus in decretales ordine alphabeti, 'Quoniam ignorans ignora-
bitur'. fol.
(*F. 144, s. xiv*)

186 Summa Godfridi super decretales et Brocarda. fol.
(*F. 7, s. xiii*)

187 Decretales cum glossa. fol.
(*F. 59, s. xiii*)

188 Decretales cum glossa anon. fol.
(*F. 150, s. xiii ex.*)

189 Decretales rursus cum glossa. fol.
(*Sent to Westminster, No. 15*)

190 Glossarium seu breve dictionarium. 8vo
(*Q. 25, s. xiii²*)

191 Summa introductoria Bonagwyde | et multa alia notabilia in decreta et
decretales. fol. litle
(*F. 146, s. xiii ex.*)

192 Isidorus de originibus. 8vo rec.

193 Summa confessorum. fol.
(*F. 113, s. xiii/xiv*)

194 Summa Reymundi de casibus libris quatuor, in fine est Berengarii
episcopi summa vide an illud sit ejus cognomen. fol.
(*F. 127, s. xiv*)

195* Summa confessorum Joh. Lectoris. fol.
(*F. 62, s. xiv in.*)

196 Summa in foro ecclesiastico Magistri Joh. de Bononia | Item summa dictaminum Thomæ de Capua. 4to
(Q. 62, s. xiv in.)

197 Rationale divinorum officiorum. Init. 'Quæcunque in ecclesiasticis officiis'. fol.
(F. 129, s. xiv)

198 Tractatus juris alphabetice. fol.
(F. 151, s. xiv)

p. 29, col. 2

199 Summa Godfridi super titulis decretalium. fol.
(F. 17, now missing)

200 Tractatus de legibus et consuetudinibus regni Angliæ tempore Henrici regis 2i compositus justitiæ gubernacula tenente Ran. de Glanvill juris regni et antiquarum consuetudinum peritissimo. Initium 'Regiam potestatem non solum armis' | sequitur tractatus de legibus et consuetudinibus Angliæ tempore magni regis Willelmi. Initium 'Post quartum annum adquisitionis regis W. istius terræ consilio baronum suorum' et cæt. | Item alius tractatus. Initium 'In rege qui recte regit necessaria sunt duo hæc' et cæt. Richardus Bracton est author, nomen libri est Breton. fol.
(F. 87, s. xiii²)

201 Tabula juris canonici et civilis edita a Fr. Joh. de Saxonia. fol.
(F. 15, s. xiv¹)

202 Vocabula juris anon. 'ordine alphabeti'. fol.
(F. 156, s. xiv in.)

203* Porphyrius super 5que universalia prædicamenta et libros posteriores | sophestria in usum Oxoniensium 'de quantitate et motu et aliis questiones' en papier. fol.
(F. 73, s. xiv)

204 Concordantia discordantium canonum. Initium 'Humanum genus duobus regitur'. fol.
(F. 120, s. xiii med.)

205 Idem liber rursus. fol.
(Sent to Westminster, No. 16)

206 Repertorium Magistri Gul. Durandi | Item libellus à Magistro Gul. de Mandagoto archidiacono de electionibus | Item apostillæ Bernardi Compostolani | et Martini repertorium, 'Inter alia quæ ad fidelium Christi doctrinam'. fol.
(F. 111, s. xiv)

207 Rofredus super actionibus in foro ecclesiastico | in fine est
　　　　　　Explicit hic bellus Ranfredi forte libellus
　　　　　　Hunc possidenti veniant bona sæpe tuenti. fol.
(F. 125, s. xiv)

---

200 *A star against this entry.*
206 *The words* super electionibus faciendis. Initium 'Hactenus ut loquar cum senecta meam ignorantiam ignoraui', et cæt. *are lined through after* archidiacono.

208   Summa Papiæ vocabulistæ.   fol.
(*F. 20, s. xiii ex.*)

209   Apparatus domini Guidonis supra extravagantes Joh. papæ.   fol.
(? *F. 168, s. xiv*)

210   Concordantiæ pars a litera F ad J.   fol.
(*F. 175, s. xiv¹*)

211   Breviarium extravagantium Bernardi prępositi Papiensis.   fol.
(*F. 122, s. xiii*)

p. 30, col. 1

212   Idem breviarium Bernardi nota ex hoc codice alia excisa.   fol.
(? *F. 177, s. xiii*)

213   Idem rursus.   fol.
(*Sent to Westminster, no. 17*)

214* Joh. Newnam de jure can[on]ico. Initium 'Omne jus aut divinum
est aut humanum'.   fol. litle
(*Q. 43, s. xiii¹*)

215* Liber juris canonici in quo habentur distinctiones et historiæ quædam
item causæ 36 sine initio.   4to
(*Q. 70, s. xii ex.*)

216* Regula Benedicti, 'Ausculta o fili præcepta Magistri' | liber scriptus
majusculis characteribus, vetus.   fol. bon.
(*Bodleian, Hatton 48, s. viii*)

217   Smaragdi abbatis expositio in regulam Benedicti. Initium 'Cum turbas
plurimorum cernerem monachorum'.   fol. bon.
(*Bodleian, Hatton 40, s. xii*)

218* De arte grammatica tractatus quidam | 1ᵘˢ 'Videndum est quid sit ars
grammatica et quæ circa ipsam sint consideranda' | 2ᵘˢ 'Ad majorem artis
grammaticæ cognitionem primo videndum est' et cęt. | Petri Blesensis epistolę
quædam | Gaufridus abbas Burtoniæ de vita Sanctæ virginis Moduennæ, 'Qui
desideraveram æstuans animo reperire' et cæt. | fragmenta quædam anonyma
in jure, theologia et geometria 'inscribitur leges Bealwardi imperf.'.   4to imperf.
(*B.M., Royal 15 B. iv, s. xii/xiii*)

219   Epistolæ Ivonis Carnotensis.   4to bon.
(*Q. 1, s. xii*)

220   Themata festivitatum sanctorum et pro tempore totius anni | Itinerarium
mentis in deum, 'Sciendum est' et cæt.   4to rec.
(*Q. 53, s. xiii ex.*)

221   Ex synodis excerpta vel potius ex multis compilatio in unum. Initium,
'Synodorum exemplarium innumerositatem conspiciens ac plurimorum ex ipsis
obscuritatem' et cæt. dividitur in titulos 69 primus est de episcopo: postremus
de variis causis | canones apostolorum | Excerpta de libr[is] Romanorum et

---

210 *MS.* and *for* ad.

Francorum, 'Si quid homicidium' | Canones Adomani. Initium 'Marina animalia ad littora delata quorum mortes nescimus sumenda sunt sana fide nisi sint putrida'. 2us 'Pecora de rupe cadentia si sanguis eorum effusus sit: sin vero sed fracta sint et sanguis foras non fluxerit refundanda sunt ut morticina' | Institutionum liber primus | Apostolorum canones 'seu' Canones concilii Nicæni et quorumdam aliorum conciliorum. vetus.   fol. bon.
(*Bodleian, Hatton 42, s. ix*)

222   Collationes decem Joh. heremitæ ad papam Leontium et Helladium fratrem. Initium 'Debitum quod beatissimo papæ Castorio' et cæt. | Bedæ expositio in Tobiam. Initium 'Liber sancti patris Tobiæ et in superficie literæ salubris patet legentibus' et cæt. | Paschalis papæ litera clero et populo Baiocensi de Turoldo epi*scopo* ab epi*scopa*tu deponendo qui illum contra canones invaserat.   fol. bon.
(*Bodleian, Hatton 23, s. xi*)

p. 30, col. 2

223   De officio missæ char*actere* saxonico.   4to bon.
(*Bodleian, Hatton 93, s. viii/ix*)

224   Quotlibeta doctoris subtilis. multa desiderantur et excisa sunt.   fol.
(*F. 60, s. xiv*)

225*   Summa Paris*iensis* de vitiis 'septem'. Initium 'Dicturi de vitiis' et cæt. | deinde de virtutibus. Initium 'Postquam dictum est de morbis ipsius animæ' et cæt. | Summula cujusdam Joh*annis* de abstinentia baptismo et cæt. ordine alphabeti | Speculum juniorum ex diversis Patrum et philosophorum libris | Liber provincialis in quo ostenditur quot sint provinciæ sub Rom*ano* pontifice | Summa de dispensationibus epi*scopo*rum abbatum et p*resbyter*orum | Proverbia Senecæ | Libri decretalium et decretorum.   fol.
(*F. 38, s. xiv in.*)

226   Quæstiones quædam physicæ de anima et aliis Walteri de Burley.   4to
(*Q. 38, s. xiii²*)

227*   Scotus super Quotlibeta. Item Kekeley in eadem. imperf.   fol.
(*F. 3, s. xiv in.*)

228*   Summa pœnitentiæ anonym. spoylde in the beginning | Item summa matrimonii, 'Quoniam frequenter in foro pœnitentiali' et cæt. In dorso est 'Raymundi summa'.   4to
(*Q. 98, s. xiii*)

229   Beda de arte metrica.   8vo bon. sed male habitus a pluvia
(*Q. 5, s. x ex.*)

230   Porphyrius super quin*que* universalia Isagoge 'categ*oriæ* periermeni*æ* Boetii divis*io* et topica' Libri posteriorum et cæt. et cæt.   4to
(*Q. 30, s. xiii*)

231   Quæstiones quædam de rebus naturalibus | summa Petri cornubiensis in logicam et sophestriam Aristot*elis* | Quæstiones 8 librorum physicorum per

---

221 *After* seu *the words* Regulæ ecclesiastice Clementis *are lined through.*
222 heremitæ *underlined.*   225 septem *substituted for* et virtutibus, *which is lined through.*

M*agistr*um Joh. de Aston, et metaphysicę ejusdem | Divisio scientiarum per
Joh. Daco Paris*iensis* et cæt.   4to rec.
(*Q. 13, s. xiii²*)

232* Sophismata Heytisbury sine principio | proportiones Bourrewill.
                                                                    fol. imperf.

(*F. 116, s. xiv ex.*)

233* Aristotelis logica.   fol.

(*F. 165, s. xiii*)

234 Porphyrii 5q*ue* universalia. categor*iæ* periermen*iæ* | et cæt. | Gilbertus
Porretanus super sex principia.   fol.

(*F. 66, s. xiii*)

Hic ultimus est in infimo subsellio unde regressus ad quartum pluteum superioris
subsellii.

p. 31, col. 1

In quarto pluteo superioris subsellii incipiendo à dextris ad sinistram.

235 Sermones de virginibus, 'Simile est regnu*m* celorum homini qui *seminavit*
bonum semen in a*gro suo*' et cæt.   fol. litle

236 Sermones Jacobi Januensis 'ep*iscopi*' dominicales | tractatus exemplorum
ordine alphab*eti*. Initium 'Antiquorum patrum exemplo didici nonnullos ad
virtutes fuisse inductos narrationibus ædificatoriis et exemplis' | vocatur alpha-
betum narrationum. nota ex præf. eundem auctorem ex auctoritatibus patrum
alium librum compilasse quem alphabetum authoritatum vocavit | tractatus
de nativitate et concept*ione* et purific*atione* Virg*inis Mariæ* | Alphabetum decre-
torum et decretalium quod Martiniana vocatur | Item moralis tractatus de
oculo, 'Si diligenter voluerimus in lege d*o*mini meditari' et cæt.   fol.

(*F. 115, s. xiv*)

237 Sermones Henrici Foukes.   8vo

(*Q. 64, s. xiii/xiv*)

238 Manipulus florum M*agistr*i Thomę de Sorbona Hybernensis.   8vo

(*Q. 23, s. xiv²*)

239 Sermones anon. Initium 'Exequutis inspirante d*o*mino sex partibus
tractatus cujus est titulus de conditione doctoris, restat pars septima' et cæt. 8vo

(*Q. 57, s. xiii ex.*)

240* Regimen animarum, liber anno 1343 scriptus. Initium 'O vos omnes
sacerdotes qui laboratis onerati et curati animarum estis' | compilatus est hic
liber ex summa summarum Reymundi, et parte oculi sacerdotis et summa
`confessorum veritatis theologiæ.   fol.

(*Bodleian, Hatton 11, s. xv in.*)

241 Fasciculus morum, ex diversis, tractatu scilicet de virt*utibus* et vitiis, ex
Elegii libro de mirabilibus mundi | et tractatu Nicholai de Furno qui est ordine
alphab*eti*.   fol.

(*F. 19, s. xv in.*)

---

235 *MS.* qui s. s. s. in a. s.
236 ep*iscopi* *interlined above* pro tempore, *which is lined through.*
239 *In margin is* Vide supra.

242* Rosarium theologiæ ordine alph*abeti*. Initium ab Absolutione | nota in initio hujus libri fuisse prophetias Hernerici sed desiderantur. 8vo
(*Q. 15, s. xv*)

243 Speculum sacerdotium 'sive vitæ beatitudo'. Initium 'Quoniam sicut dicit apostolus' et cęt. 8vo
(*Q. 22, s. xiv ex.*)

244 Via vel dieta salutis. Init*ium* 'Hæc est via ambulate in ea' | tractatus de oculo spirituali et morali, 'Si diligenter voluerimus in lege d*omi*ni meditari'. 8vo
(*Q. 14, s. xiv ex.*)

245 Veritas Theologiæ. Initium 'Veritatis theologiæ sublimitas' et cæt. Item comment. in sententias. fol.
(*F. 2, s. xiv in.*)

246 Tractatus de diversis materiis prædicabilibus in septem partes tributus juxta 7 dona Spir*itus* Sancti. Initium 'Quoniam multi multipliciter subtiliter et utiliter elaboraverunt'. 4to
(*Q. 85, s. xiii ex.*)

p. 31, col. 2

247 Legendæ Sanctorum Jac. Januensis, 'Diversum tempus pręsentis vitæ in quatuor distinguitur'. fol.
(*F. 45, s. xiv in.*)

248 Rursus. fol. litle
(*Sent to Westminster, No. 18*)

249 Vita S*anc*ti Pauli heremitæ, Antonii et Hilarionis auth*ore* Hieronymo 'bon.' | ejusdem narrationes eorum quæ de Hierosylimis in Ægyptum pergens vidit. Initium 'Benedictus Deus qui vult omnes homines salvos fieri'. fol. bon.
(*F. 48, s. xi med.*)

250 Liber de abstinentia: ita inscribitur quia ejus initium est ab abstinentia. videtur liber distinctionum ordine enim alph*abeti* procedit ad finem usq*ue* | commune Sanctorum sive adaptationes omnium sermonum dominicalium et festivalium | de miseria condit*ionis* human*æ* Lotharius diac*onus* card*inalis* postea Innocent*ius* 3*us*. Item meditationes Bernardi de interiori homine. fol.
(*F. 117, s. xiii–xiii/xiv*)

251 De caussa dei contra Pelagium Thomas de Bredewardina Lond*inensis* cancellariu*m* (*sic*). fol.
(*F. 112, s. xiv*)

252 Liber precum in festis S*anc*torum. 4to

253* Aldelmus de virginitate charactere saxonico. 4to imperf.
(*Royal 5 F. iii, s. ix/x*)

254 Albertus de natura locorum | de cælo et mundo | idem in logicam | tractatus Joh. Dumbleton de terminis et cæt. fol.
(*F. 23, s. xiv*)

---

242 Henrici *altered to* Hernerici.

255　Aristotelis metaphysica cum glossa.　　　　　　　　　fol.
(*F. 18, s. xiv in.*)

256　Burleius de potentiis animæ et de sensibus interioribus et exterioribus |
tractatus Magistri Scharpe de anima quæstionative et in 8 libros physicorum |
idem de passionibus entis | Burleyus de duobus principiis | tractatus de terminis
relativis | item alius de Iride, qui vocatur propter mirari | de finito et infinito
tractatus | Scoti quæstiones in Meteorologica | quæstiones Joh. Dedeci in Ethica |
quæstiones Antonii in Metaphysica.　　　　　　　　　　　fol.
(*F. 86, s. xv*)

257　Concilium Ottoboni legati celebratum Londini | summa Joh. doctoris
in quartum sententiarum.　　　　　　　　　　　　　　　fol.

258　Sententiæ veraces Sancti Thomæ in Ethica.　　　　　　fol.
(*F. 138, s. xiv*)

259　Albertus in 8 libros physicorum | Metaphysica 'secundum veterem
tralationem' cum commento | textus physicorum et cæt.　　　　fol.
(*F. 42, s. xiii*)

260　Ethica Aristotelis.　　　　　　　　　　　　　　　　fol.
(*F. 63, s. xiii/xiv*)

261　Averrois in 8 libros physicorum et in libros de generatione et corrup-
tione. absunt ejus comment. in libros de gen. et corrupt. per plagiarium
ablati.　　　　　　　　　　　　　　　　　　　　　　fol.
(*F. 96, s. xiv*)

p. 32, col. 1

262　Meteorologicων libri quatuor | epitome Romanæ historiæ Flori | Macrobius
in somnium scipionis | tractatus de decem præceptis Fr. Henrici de Vrimaria
ordinis Fr. heremitarum Sancti Augustini. Initium 'Audi Israel præcepta
domini et cet. In verbis istis propositis' et cæt. en papier.　　fol. rec.
(*F. 68, s. xiv²*)

263　Comment. in libros de anima '3bus libris'. Initium 'Dixit Aristoteles
Quoniam de rebus honorabilibus' et cæt. Item de substantia corporis tractatus
ad cujus finem est Averrois nomen, forte idem est author prioris tractatus.
Initium posterioris est 'Intendimus in hoc tractatu perscrutari'.　4to
(*Q. 34, s. xiii/xiv*)

264*　Wyvesched (*sic*) de motu locali et aliis, en papier recens.　fol.
(*F. 35, s. xv*)

265*　Quæstiones in Metaphysica.　　　　　　　　　　4to imperf.
(*Q. 90, s. xiii/xiv*)

266　Comment. in libros Metaphysicorum | Item de ideis et unitatibus liber. fol.
(*F. 4, s. xiii*)

267　Metaphysica et Ethica Aristotelis.　　　　　　　　　fol.
(*F. 169, s. xiv in.*)

268　Liber medicinæ a Gilberto anglico compositus.　　　　fol.
(*F. 145, s. xiv in.*)

269* Tractatus de caussis et principiis naturalibus. Init*ium* 'Expedivimus nos auxilio Dei' | Item in libros de anima Israelitæ phi*losophi* inscribitur Johanni Toletano (*sic*) epi*scopo* | cum aliis anonymorum aliorum tractatibus in philo-so*phi*a. 4to
(*Q. 81, s. xiii*[1]*–xiii med.*)

270 Ars medicinæ sive regalis dispositio Hali filii abbæ (*sic*) discipuli Abimeher Moysi filii Seyar ex arabico interprete Stephano ph*ilosophi*æ discipulo. fol.
(*F. 40, s. xii med.*)

271 Catonis disticha | Theodulus | Claudianus de raptu proserpinæ in principio mutilus | Doctrinale, 'Scribere clericulis paro doctrinale novellis Pluraq*ue* doctoru*m* sociabo scripta meorum' et cæt. | de grammatica et prosodia est tractatus | Anticlaudianus | Alexandreis | Horatii odæ primus liber excissus est alia item ejusdem sed imperfecta et mutila | Juvenalis | Persius | Liber qui dicitur Chartula ab initio, 'Chartula nostra tibi portat dilecte salutes Multa videbis ibi si non hæc dona refutes' et cæt. | Urban*us* liber tractatus est de morum urbanitate unde nomen, 'Moribus ornari si vis lector venerari' et cæt. | Lucanus 'integer'. liber recenti manu scriptus non tamen malus in perg. fol.
(*F. 147, s. xiii*)

272 Isagoge Johanicii ad technen Galeni | Theophilus de urinis | Constantinus de febribus | Isaac de urinis | Ægidius de eisdem metrice item et de pulsibus et cæt. fol.
(*F. 85, s. xiii*)

p. 32, col. 2

273 Passionarius liber est de medicina. 4to
(*Q. 40, s. xii*)

274 Tractatus in medicina sine initio et fine recentioris cujusdam. 4to
(*Q. 96, s. xiii*)

275* Gerardinus de modo medendi | flores dietarum et cæt. anon. 8vo
(*Cf. Appendix III, no. 9*)

276 Viaticum Constantini Africani | Isaac de urinis | dietæ universales | et cæt. fol. litle
(*Q. 41, s. xiii*)

277 Decem libri Pantegni qui vocantur theorica Constantini montis Cassinensis monachi. fol.
(*F. 70, s. xiii*)

278 Comment. Hali super tegni Galeni. 4to
(*Q. 49, s. xiii*)

279 Almansor ita dictus [eo quod] regis Mansoris præcepto scriptus sit ab Albubeenazari filii Zachariæ | Item synonyma Rasy. 4to
(*Q. 60, s. xiii*[1])

280 Herbale ordine alphabeti. Initium 'Circa instans negotium de simplicibus' | Item antidotarium. Initium 'Liber iste quem in præsentiarum' | tabulæ Salerni cum commento | Yeraldus in fine ita, in initio autem Geraudus. Initium 'Cum omnis scientia ex fine et utilitate' et cæt. 4to
(*Q. 52, s. xiii*)

281 Theorica Constantini Africani et Galeni quædam.   fol.
(*Q. 39, s. xiii*)

282 Brito Vocabularius.   fol.
(*Sent to Westminster, No. 19*)

283 Vocabularius alter seu magnę derivationes Hugutii.   fol.
(*F. 22, s. xiii ex.*)

284 Brito rursus   in initio sunt quidam rythmi 'Difficiles studeo partes quas biblia gestat Pandere sed nequeo latebras nisi qui manifestat' et cæt.   fol.
(*F. 13, s. xiii–xiv in.*)

285 Mythologia Alexandri, in fine tractatus additur etiam nomen Albricii | summa de virtutibus antiquorum principum et philosophorum, 'Quoniam misericordia et veritas custodiunt regem' | Valerius ad Ruffinum contra nuptias | Comment. 'Rydwaus' in Fulgentii mythologiam. Initium 'Intentio venerabilis viri Fulgentii in sua mytho*logia*' | Quintiliani declamationes | epistola Bernardi ad Cunrhadum epi*scopu*m, et comment. ejusdem in Theodolum | et cæt. non magni mome*n*ti.   fol.
(*F. 154, s. xiv ex.*)

286 Vita Sa*n*ctorum Barlaam et Josaphat | Galfridus Monumetensis | Tractatus de terrę partibus et provinciis vide an sit Huntundinensis. Initium 'De terræ autem partibus et diversis provinciis per quas orbis est generaliter divisus, pauca huic operi adjuvante deo sunt breviter inserenda' et cæt. | Beda de verborum figuris.   8vo
(*B.M., Harley 5394*)

p. 33, col. 1

287 Compendiloquium de vita et dictis illustrium philosophorum, 'Cum igitur (*sic*) debeamus apes imitari' et cæt. | tractatus de vitio linguæ | synonima Isidori et cæt.   spoyled with rayne.   fol. litle
(*Q. 72, s. xiv med.*)

288 Osberti grammatica inscripta Glocestriæ abbati Thamelino (*? sic, for* Hamelino).   4to
(*Q. 37, s. xiii²*)

289 Grammatica Petri Helie.   caret initio liber videtur bonus.   fol. bon.
(*F. 99, s. xiii¹*)

290 Tractatus de re grammatica. Initium 'Philosophia genus [est] cæterarum disciplinarum' | ars algorismi et cæt.   fol.
(*F. 123, s. xiv*)

291 Grammatica Prisciani. bon.   4to
(*This or 292 is Royal 15 B. xiv (s. xii ex.) or sent to Westminster, No. 20*)

292 Rursus eadem.   4to bon.
(*This or 291 is Royal 15 B. xiv or sent to Westminster, No. 20*)

293* De virtute lapidum tractatus carmine, 'Evax rex Arabum' et cæt. | tractatus in grammatica, 'Qui bene vult disponere familiæ suæ' et cæt.   4to
(*Q. 58 in 1697 catalogue, now missing*)

---

286 *A star against this entry.*   290 ars algorismi *lined through.*

294* Grammatica anon., 'Ad majorem artis grammaticæ cognitionem' et cæt. | de constructione Petrus Helie. Initium 'Absoluta cujuslibet disciplinę perfectio duplici comparatur exercitio' et cæt. forte idem author est prioris tractatus quod etiam ex collatione superioris exemp*laris* patet.   fol.
(*F. 137, s. xiv in.*)

295 Quæstiones quædam in prædicamenta et sermones quidam 'papier'. fol. rec.
(*F. 65, s. xiv/xv*)

296* Liber grammaticalis, 'Qui bene vult disponere' et cæt.   4to

297 Missale cum notis musicis item psalterium.   4to

298 Missale aliud cum notis musicis.   4to

299 Euclidis initium | et sermones anon.   8vo
(*Q. 89, s. xiii ex.*)

300 Homiliarium, 'Abjiciamus opera tenebrarum', et cæt. | liber est lacer et male habitus a pluvia et plagiario.   fol.
(*F. 157, s. xiii²*)

301 Homilia anon. spoyled.   4to

302 Precationes quædam seu missalis pars.   fol. litle
(*Q. 26, s. xiv*)

303 Distinctiones ut videntur theologiæ ordine alphabeti, 'Antiquorum patrum exemplo didici' et cæt. vide supra. spoyled.   4to
(*Q. 97, s. xiv*)

p. 33, col. 2

304* Sophistria secundum usum Oxoniensem | Item tractatus Joh. Milverley de quantitate et qualitate. en papier.   fol.
(*F. 118, s. xiv/xv*)

305* Commentum 'seu potius glossa' Duncaht pontificis Hiberniensis quod contulit suis discipulis in monasterio S*an*cti Remigii docens super astrologia Capellæ Varronis Martiani.   8vo
(*Royal 15 A. xxxiii, s. x in.*)

306* De prædicamentis | de syllogismo et cæt.   fol.
(*F. 119, s. xiii²*)

307 Gesta romanorum | Seneca de remediis fortuitorum | tractatus de vitiis capitalibus qui vocatur metaphora creaturarum | de nuptiis spiritualibus. Initium 'Flagitastis fratres charissimi' | parvum bonum Bonaventuræ | epistolæ Mason, 'Post primi parentis culpam derivatam in posteros' | speculum peccatorum, 'Quoniam charissime in hujus vitæ via' | item qu*e*dam 'distinctiones'. fol.
(*F. 80, s. xv*)

308 Vetus logica et nova. Initium 'Abstractum est in genere' et cæt.   fol.
(*F. 72, s. xiv¹*)

309* Precationes quædam charactere saxonico.   4to
(? *Royal 2 A. xx, s. viii*)

---

305 *A cross against this entry.*

310*   Gul. Milverley super 5*que* universalia | et Wehoedale (*sic*) super eadem | Alyngto*n* in prædicamenta | et Milverley de principiis sex.   8vo
(*Q.54, s. xv*)

311   Pars oculi   all spoyld. Initium 'Cum ecclesiæ quibus præficiuntur per-sonæ'.   8vo
(*Q.92, s. xiv*)

312   Distinctiones (ut videntur) quædam theologicæ   all spoyld.   8vo
(? *Q. 18, s. xiii ex.–xiv*)

313   Comment. in libros Aristo*telis* Priorum. Initium 'Quæ sit auctoris in-tentio in hoc opere quis finis' et cæt.   4to
(*Q.58, s. xiii in.*)

314   Homiliæ quædam lacerę.   4to
(? *Q. 100, s. xiv in.*)

315   Quæstiones quædam theologicæ laceræ et imperf.   fol.
(? *Q.99, s. xiii/xiv*)

316   Fragmentum passionum quorumdam Sa*n*ctorum   quyte spoyled.   fol.

p. 34, col. 1
Libri Saxonici

317   Sermones in Hexameron | de dominica ora*tione* | fide catholica | de die judicii | de auguriis | de doctrina apostolica | de dilectione dei et proximi | de visionibus Frusei (*sic*) | de visionibus Drithelmi | de efficacia missæ | de cogita-tione | de martyribus | de virginibus | de dedicatione eccl*esiæ* | de 12 abusivis secundum Cyprianu*m* et cæt.   8vo
(*Bodleian, Hatton 115, s. xi ex.*)

318–19 Sermones 'inter quos quidam sunt Lupi ep*iscopi*', Be ðam frum-sceafte | de fide | de baptismo | de visione Isaiæ | de antichristo | de christiani-tate | de temporibus antichristi | de falsis diis | de baptismo | de cæna domini | de letania majore | de antichristo | de sacerdotio et cæt. numero 62 postremu[s] est de dedicatione ecclesiæ 2bus vol. elegantissime scriptis. describe epistolam Cardinalium Roma*norum* ad Wlstanum in initio primi tomi, "J. et P. pres-by*teri* Card*inales* missi a papa Alexandro ad reformationem ecclesiæ anglicanæ Wlstanum rogant per literas ut cum omnibus abbatibus dioc*esis* suæ interesse velit concilio ad Wincestram tertia die post Pascha".   4to litle
(*Bodleian, Hatton 113, 114, s. xi*)

320   Sermones in natalibus Sa*n*ctorum Ceaddæ | Joh. Baptistæ | de passione Petri et Pauli | commemoratio Pauli | de passione Laurenti (*sic*) | de assump*tione* Virg*inis* | de pass*ione* Bartholo*mei* | de decollatione Joh. Baptist*æ* | de nativita*te* Mari*ę* | de sancta virginitate | in natale Sa*n*cti Andreæ | et Sa*n*cti Clementis | et cæt.   4to
(*Bodleian, Hatton 116, s. xii*)

318–19 *The words* inter…*episcopi* *are substituted for* Lupi episcopi *which are lined through. The words* 'J. et P.…*.Pascha*' *are in the margin.*

321 Constitutiones lingua saxonica de episcopis | de synodo | de sacerdotibus | sinodalia decreta | de gradibus ecclesiasticis | de officiis diurnalium et nocturnalium horarum | de matitunali (*sic*) officio | de prima hora | de officio tertiæ horæ | et sextæ | ad nonam | ad vesperam | ad completorium | de nocturnali celebratione | de regula canonicorum | de peccatis multis judicium | quomodo judicantur epi*scopi* pres*byte*ri et diaconi | de paganis quomodo nubant et de eis qui per ignor*antiam* bis baptizati sunt | de infantibus non baptizatis | de pres*byte*ro non baptizato | de monachis et sanctimonialibus | de sacrificiis quæ dæmoniis immolantur | de juramento | de operibus diei dominici et eucharistia et ministratione | de eucharistia perdita | de cibo sanctificato et his qui immunda gustant et cæt. Nota in initio esse capitula concilii celebrati apud Winceastriam præsente pontificis legato Ermenfredo epi*scopo* Sedunensi anno domini 1086 Ind*ictione* 14ta (*sic*) temporibus W. regis et Lanfranci archiepi*scopi*.
(*Bodleian, Junius 121, s. xi*)

p. 34, col. 2

322 Dialogi Gregorii translati ab Ælfredo in linguam saxonicam imperf. | Liber medicinalis sive herbarum descriptio et vires 'lingua item saxonica' | De nominibus et virtutibus lapid*um* qui in orientis partibus inveniuntur et qui in medicinæ artem recipiuntur. Nota præfigi duas epistolas Evacis Arabiæ regis quas Tiberio Imp. misit. Initium operis est ab Adamante, 'Adamas igitur est lapis colore ferrugineus splendore christallinus durior ferro et optimus, nascitur in India' et cæt. soluta oratione non carmine. fol. bon.
(*Bodleian, Hatton 76, s. xi*)

323 Egesippi ni fallor historiæ, initio caret sed 'non multa desiderantur'. primi libri finis, 'hunc finem habuit Herodes'. Secundi initium, 'Sepulto Herode libera ut in defunctos solent judicia populi depromebantur' | Tertii initium 'Ea postquam Neroni nunciata sunt' | Quarti, 'Extractis Tarichæis' et cæt. | Quinti 'Anno primo delati imperii' | Finis 'Una mulier sola superfuit quæ filios quinq*ue* in aquæ ductu abscondit, dum cæteri supremis intendunt necessitatibus. Ea romanis diluculo advenientibus ad vocem excita index negotii fuit; opes autem eorum appositus ab ipsis 'prius' ignis consumpsit'.
(*F. 30, s. xii med.*)   bon. fol. faire

324* Compilatio decretorum Ivonis | canones item Apostolorum et Concilia quædam elegantissime scripta sed quædam in medio excissa sunt. bon. fol. faire
(*Bodleian, Hatton 6, s. xiii in.*)

325 Fasciculus morum. Initium 'Frater noster dilecte ac sodalis prędilecte'.   8vo
(*Q. 3, s. xv*)

326 Chrysost*omus* in Matth*æum* imperf. | Bernardus in cantica | Aug. contra hæreses | idem de eleemosyna | et epistola ejusdem de orando Deum | Bernardus super Missus est angelus | Ovidius de amoris remedio.   8vo rec.
(*Q. 55, s. xiii–xiv²*)

---

321 præsente *substituted for* præsidente, *which is lined through.*
322 *Three horizontal lines after this entry, the last of the* 'Libri Saxonici'.

327   Ewandi ordinis vallis scholarium sermones dominicales.   8vo
(*Q. 87, s. xiv*)

328   Postillæ anonymi, 'Abjiciamus opera tenebrarum et induamus arma
lucis'.   8vo
(*Q. 17, s. xiii/xiv*)

329   Sermones et collationes de San*c*ta Maria et aliis. 'Ave gratia plena
Luc. 2° et sunt verba archangeli'.   8vo litle
(*Q. 63, s. xiii/xiv*)

330*   Smaragdus de diversis virtutibus, liber diadema vocatur. Initium 'Hunc
modicum op*er*is nostri libellum' et cæt.   4to bon.
(*Royal 8 D. xiii, s. xii in.*)

331   Sermones dominicales Fr. Byart. Initium 'Pręparate corda vestra
d*o*mino'.   8vo
(*Q. 4, s. xiii/xiv*)

p. 35, col. 1

332   Sermones anon. 'in Genesim', 'In principio creavit deus et cæt. In
verbis prepositis' | expositio in librum Job et cæt.   8vo
(*Q. 59, s. xiv*[1])

333*   Cypriani testimoniale ut habet inscriptio sed falso ni fallor. Initium
'Canon in hæbraica regula in græca æquitas in latina' cur æquitas dicitur video
quia plus minusve æquo vitat | sequitur tractatus alter, 'Episcopatus nomen
est oneris non honoris' etc. Videtur esse defloratio quædam canonum. 8vo mag.
(*Royal 5 E. xiii, s. ix ex.*)

334   Reportationes Joh. de Dombletone monachi Wigorn. de sermonibus
Oxoniæ, 'Benedictus qui venit in nomine d*o*mini'.   8vo mag.
(*Q. 46, s. xiii ex.*)

335   Sermones Ockham. Initium 'Veritas de terra orta est ps*almus* Veritas
ante lapsum primi hominis in terra fuit'.   8vo
(*Q. 74, s. xiii*[2])

336   Hieronymus in ecclesiasten | Beda in canticum Canticorum libris
septem, imperfect.   4to bon.
(*Q. 66, s. xii*)

337*   Sermones duo lingua saxonica primus de antichristo malefico | '2us' de
die judicii imperf. | Tractatus per interrogationes et responsiones de 7 gradibus
ecclesiasticæ dignitatis. Initium 'Dic ergo Frater gradus ecclesiastici ordinis
quot sunt?' | Albinus de fide 'et trinitate' interrog. et respo*n*. | expositio
missæ | Interrog*ationes* et respons*iones*. Initium 'Homo unde dicitur. resp.
homo dictus est ab humo quia de limo terræ formatus est'. | Isidori probatio
fidei catholicę, 'Patrem nec natum nec factum esse credo' et cæt. | Æsopi
fabulæ, imperf. præf. initium 'Romulus Tiberino filio de civitate attica. Æsopus
quidam homo gręcus et ingeniosus famulos suos docet quid homines observare
debeant' et cæt.   8vo

---

333 æquitas *underlined.*
337 duo *substituted for* quidam, *which is lined through. A star against the end of this entry.*

338 Tractatus de ambiguis theologiæ. Initium 'Agentes et consentientes pari pœna punientur' | Ex Origine (*sic*) in numeros, 12 prophetas, epistolas et acta quædam excerpta | opusculum de dubiis in evangeliis. Initium 'Omnis homo aut primus Adam aut secundus' | et sermones quidam. 4to
(*Q. 29, s. xii ex.*)

339 Retractatio Aug. contra epistolam Manichæi quam vocant Fundamentum | et retractatio contra Adamantium Manichæi discipulum | Ordinale secundum usum Sarum | et *2us* liber Aug. contra literas Petiliani. 4to rec.

p. 35, col. 2

340 Communiloquium. Initium 'Cum doctor sive prædicator evangelii' et cæt. Synonima Isidori Hispalensis | tractatus de pænis inferni | Abusiva secundum Aug. | testamentum Francisci | manuale Guidonis | tractatus de 7 sacramentis | Vita Sancti Eadmundi | meditationes Bernardi. 4to rec.
(*Q. 27, s. xiv*)

341* Sermones pœnitentium. Initium 'Qui sedes super cherubim appare coram Ephraim' et cæt. | tractatus de officiis anni. 4to lacer.
(*Q. 78, s. xii ex.*)

342* Compendium veteris testamenti editum à Magistro Petro Pictaviensi cancellario Parisiensi. Initium 'Considerans historiæ prolixitatem' et cæt. usque ad annum 1242. fol. large
(? *Eton College 96, s. xiii med.*)

343 A missall in english. 8vo

Finis τελος

Summa omnium 343

1 Anselmus Cur Deus homo | de veritate | de processione spiritus sancti | de casu diaboli | de conceptione virginali | monologion | de concordia præscientiæ prædestinationis | de prędestinatione et libero arbitrio | de gratia et libero arbitrio | de libertate arbitrii | de incarnatione verbi | de libertate verbi | de similitudinibus | disputatio inter Christianum et gentilem | de septem beatitudinibus | de felicitate justorum | de conceptione Virginis | de antichristo | de grammatico | de azimo et fermento | Anselmi epistola ad Lanfrancum item aliæ paucæ epistolæ ad alios | meditationes | quæstiones ejusdem | de sacramentis | de ortu progressu et occasu Salvatoris | de malo et nichilo | de silentio | Bernardus de dispensatione et præcepto. fol.
(*Sent to Westminster, No. 3, see above, No. 33*)

2 Anselmi, meditationes | de similitudinibus | oratio ad Joh. baptistam | prosologion | de reparatione humana | de veritate | de libertate arbitrii | de casu diaboli | de conceptione Virginis | de processione Spiritus Sancti | de concordia | de incarnatione verbi | de sacrificio | epistola de sacramentis ecclesiæ | de excellentia et conceptione Virginis | de ortu Salvatoris | de occupatione bona | disputatio inter Christianum et gentilem | de antichristo | de corpore et sanguine Christi | de sacramentis ecclesiæ | quęstiones | et epistolæ quædam. fol.
(*F. 132, see above, No. 32*)

3   Anselmus de casu diaboli | de conceptu virginali | monologion | prosologion |
contra insipientem | de concordia præscientiæ 'et prædestinationis' | cur deus
homo primus et secundus | de gratia et libero arbitrio | de incarnatione verbi | de
veritate | de processione Spiritus Sancti | de similitudinibus | de grammatico |
quæstiones | disputatio inter Christianum et gentilem | de 7 beatitudinibus | de
beata vita et felicitate justorum | de occupatione bona | de conceptione Virginis |
de excellentia Virginis | Item quædam epistolæ | meditationes | de antichristo |
de azimo et fermento | de sacrificio græcorum | de ortu et progressu Salvatoris |
epistolę de sacramentis | de malo | Sermo in illud Intravit unus (sic for Iesus)
in quoddam castellum.   fol.
(F. 41, see above, No. 34)

p. 36, col. 1

*In bibliotheca Allani Oxoniensis.
Martianus Capella cum glossa bis
Sidonius Apollinaris bis
Salustius
Ciceronis quædam
Turgotus Dunelmensis de vitis et gestis episcoporum illius sedis   4to bon.
Chronica quædam anon. Angliæ
Liber monasterii Sanctæ Frediswidæ (sic)
Constantini itinerarium cum comment. Talbot
   Reliqui omnes fere sunt mathematici et philosophici.

*In bibliotheca Graftonensi quæ est Comitis Salopiensis.
Augustini quædam '2bus vol.' et Gregorii magni et Bedæ 'aliis duobus' |
Gullielmi Barre archidiaconi Eliensis compendium Bibliorum[1] | præter glossas
in quosdam libros bibliorum præterea nihil dignum visu est: et numerus est
exiguus valde, non excedit viginti.

[p. 37 is blank]

p. 38, col. 1

Σημειωσαι reperiri in bibliotheca Cottoniana chartularium vetus Wigorn.
ecclesiæ in quo chartæ omnes antiquæ 'transcribuntur' quæ in chartophylacio
αὐτογραφαι servantur | in quo codice habetur tractatus Hemmingi monachi
Wigorn. de antiquis possessionibus illius ecclesiæ à quibus concessæ fuerint et
quorum fraude et rapina sublatæ. Vixit hic Hemmingus Sancti Wlstani tempore
cujus jussu tractatum hunc scripsit. Nota ibidem, Wlstanum antiqua omnia
testamenta et privilegia de possessionibus Wigorn. ecclesiæ diligenter investigasse
et in duobus voluminibus congregata ordinasse; in uno primitiva omnia
testamenta et privilegia in quibus donationes terrarum et possessionum manifesta-
bantur, in altero vero chirographa quibus Oswaldus archiepiscopus cum adju-
torio Edgari regis terras injuste ablatas, ecclesiæ restitui curavit post duorum
vel trium hæredum tempora, chirographorum exemplaribus in scrinio ecclesiæ

---

[1] Bibliorum substituted for scripturarum, which is lined through.

ob testimonium collocatis. quæ omnia transcribi jussit Wlstanus et in bibliotheca ecclesiæ reponi ne forte testamentales scedulæ negligentia aliqua per-
derentur vel corrumperentur. Præcepit præterea privilegia omnia et chirographa terrarum quæ proprie ad monachorum victum pertinent in duobus
voluminibus similiter et eodem ordine congregari; quod a se factum in hoc
opere pro parvitatis suæ modulo Hemmingus profitetur.[1]

p. 38, col. 2

Catalogus librorum manuscriptorum Wigorniensis Bibliothecæ.

---

[1] *Before Young wrote this notice the column contained the words* Dominus petra mea et
robur meum Artes et scientiæ ab hominibus inventæ, *which interrupt the text between*
restitui *and* curavit *and have been crossed out. The incipit is that of Holcot's commentary on
Wisdom, No. 62 above.*

NOTES

ON YOUNG'S CATALOGUE

3   Royal MS. 4 C. ii belonged to Theyer and appears to be a Worcester book, since it contains the bull 'De canonizatione reverendi patris nostri Wuulstani'. But it contains Jerome's commentary on six minor prophets only. The binding is modern.

5   Royal MS. 4 A. xiv is a companion volume to Royal MS. 2 B. v and was probably written at Winchester. Ff. 107–8, formerly used as binding leaves, contain a fragment of Felix, *Vita Sancti Guthlaci*, in Anglo-Saxon minuscule, s. viii/ix.

7   Young's description of MS. F. 25 is correct, that in the 1906 catalogue incorrect.

13   The text of Ruth, with its gloss, does not usually take up more than about one quire of a manuscript.

18   The editors of the Royal catalogue do not mention the occurrence of the verses in Royal MS. 5 C. ii and it has not been possible to see the manuscript. The verses occur in Royal MS. 13 B. vi and in Worcester Cathedral MS. Q. 48: they refer to the death of Richard I. 'salutis' should be 'Calucis'.

22   Fulbert's letter to R., abbot of St Médard (*Patr. Lat.* 141. 244, Ep. 91) is listed by Casley among the contents of Royal MS. 5 A. xiii, but is omitted from the description in the 1921 catalogue. The manuscript contains the press-mark C. xiii on fol. 1ᵛ.

23   The only known manuscripts of the 'Disputatio regalis Alcuini et Pippini' appear to be Wolfenbüttel, Herzog-August Bibliothek MS. 4638 (Gudianus lat. 4⁰ 331) from the Gottorp library, and Vienna, Nazional-bibliothek MS. 808 from Salzburg. The text is printed from the former in *Patr. Lat.* 101. 975 and from the latter in *Zeitschrift für deutsches Altertum*, xiv (1869), 531.

28   The letter referred to is printed in *Patr. Lat.* 22, Ep. 62.

29   Richard of St Victor, *De trinitate*, occurs in MS. F. 32, ff. 293–313ᵛ, and is included in the description of that manuscript given in MS. Tanner 268 and in the 1697 catalogue, but is not noticed in the 1906 catalogue or by Schenkl, *Bibliotheca Patrum Latinorum Britannica* (1891).

31   MS. Q. 24, ff. 188–90, contains a table 'super temporale Omeliarum Magistri Odonis'.

34   The 'De occupatione bona' occupies two leaves of MS. F. 41 between the articles numbered 17 and 18 in the 1906 catalogue.

37   Glasgow, Hunterian MS. V. 5. 1 (431) contains notes which are un-mistakably in the 'tremulous' Worcester hand.

41   By 'vestigiis plagii' Young means perhaps stubs showing where leaves had been cut or torn out. The manuscript is not at present available for inspection. It has been rebound since Young wrote.

43   MS. Q. 51 contains on ff. 51–8 two letters from St Bernard to Pope Innocent, both directed against Peter Abaelard: the first begins 'Oportet ad

vestrum' (*Patr. Lat.* 182. 1053, Ep. 190) and the second 'Necesse est ut veniant scandala' (*Patr. Lat.* 182. 354, Ep. 189).

47   The commentary is duly ascribed to Jerome in the text of MS. F. 83, but a faint title written on the second cover appears to read 'Bedæ'. A label formerly pasted over this title is now lost. The title given to the manuscript in MS. Tanner 268, 'Bedæ Presbyteri expositio in Marcum Evangelistam', no doubt reproduces the inscription on the label.

50   The medieval table of contents of MS. F. 57 lists 'Quedam epistole anselmi' after 'De magistro' (art. 21 in the 1906 catalogue). The medieval paging springs from 338 to 345 at this point, showing that three leaves have been removed after the present f. 173.

51   The incipit of the text beginning on f. 88 of MS. F. 84 is '*Quam pulchri sunt gressus tui in calceamentis* filia principis. can. 7. Diuine sapiencie summa et incomprehensibilis et inscrutabilis prouidencia.' The letters printed in italics are missing, since the whole of the upper margin and most of the first line of text have been destroyed by damp. The leaf was evidently in the same condition in Young's time as it is now. The title 'Postilla fratris Hugonis de Birlingam in Exodum', adopted in the 1906 catalogue, is written in the margin of f. 88 in a hand of s. xvii. There is no other title in the manuscript. Young's title, which appears to be correct, was derived probably from a label on the second cover, which has been lost in rebinding. The cataloguer in MS. Tanner 268 appears to have found difficulty in reading this label, since he copied only the words 'Postilla fratris Hugonis'. For Hugh of Bressingham, O.F.M., see *English Historical Review*, XLIX (1934), 673–6. The postils are in 40 chapters.

55   The description would apply to MS. F. 162 or to Bodleian MS. Auct. D. inf. 2. 4 (*S.C.* 4089), but it seems not unlikely that the former is a seventeenth-century addition to the collection at Worcester.

68   The medieval label of MS. Q. 94, formerly on the second cover and now on the end pastedown, reads 'Euangelium Johannis cum glossa'.

72   The title on a label on the second cover of MS. F. 21 is 'Rabanus de naturis rerum'. The same title is on the backstrip of the binding.

77   Schenkl, who gives a full account of MS. F. 94, does not mention the homily beginning on f. 224 'Supereminentem omni quod post hominem deum creatum est', the title of which, in a hand of s. xiv, is 'Anselmus de excellentia beate virginis'. An older title has been erased. The homily is by Eadmer and is printed in *Patr. Lat.* 159. 557.

78   Patristic sources, 'Amb'', 'Aug'', 'Gg'', etc. are noted in red ink in the margins of MS. F. 143.

80   The thirteenth-century table of contents of MS. F. 71 describes art. 10 of the 1906 catalogue as 'Tractatus Magistri Ricardi s. Qui bene presunt presbiteri'. The author is usually identified with Richard Wethershed.

96   The 'Tractatus de octo partibus orationis', with incipit 'Effectum grammatice', begins on f. 193ᵛ of MS. F. 61. The piece 'De figuris vel tropis locucionum', ascribed in the manuscript to Cassiodorus, but really by Bede, is on ff. 167–8ᵛ. The title 'Promatheus' is written on the backstrip of the binding and 'promotheus' is in a hand of s. xv at the head of f. 1. These titles are derived from art. 1, the 'Promatheus' of Rogerus Compotista, monk of

Bury.[1] The running title on ff. 2, 3 appears to have given rise to the absurd ascription to St Jerome in the 1906 catalogue. Young's note, 'Prometheus Huberti monachi', is presumably derived from something in his no. 103 which is now missing.

98 The name 'Thomas Grene' (s. xv ex.) is scribbled on a flyleaf of MS. Barlow 4. The same name in the same hand occurs in MS. Q. 17 at Worcester. It is also in Royal MS. 8 D. xiii, a Worcester manuscript.

99 The headings quoted by Young occur on ff. 271–83 of MS. F. 126.

102 Bodleian MS. Hatton 102 (*S.C.* 4051) contains the 'De decem preceptis per fratrem Johannem de Rupella'. The treatise is usually anonymous.

107 On the last flyleaf (f. 336) of MS. F. 10 there is an inscription in which consonants are substituted for vowels: normalized it reads 'Iste liber constat dompno tome meldenham'. Meldenham was prior from 1499 to 1507. The title in MS. Tanner 268, 'Sermones Weldenhami (*sic*) Wigorniæ', may be derived from a scribble on f. 336 or from a lost label.

111 The inscription on the old label of MS. Q. 11 is 'Sermones nonnulli de diuersis festis et dominicis'.

112 Young's reference is to no. 40 in his catalogue of the St Paul's Cathedral manuscripts (see above, p. 1), 'Sermones Blesensis, initium Emitte manum tuam et cæt. Ecce charissimi sicut naufragi in medium fluctuum'.

114 MS. Q. 45 is called 'Postilla Guiberti Bedmisteri' on a flyleaf and in MS. Tanner 268. The title is probably taken from a (misread?) label, now lost. 'Willelmus Bedmystre' was the scribe: he wrote also Bodleian MS. Bodley 795 (*S.C.* 2644) at Oxford in 1435, and Brit. Mus., Royal MS. 10 A. xviii.

123 The title on f. 38 of MS. Q. 67 is 'Sermones fratris Ricardi de Theford', for whom see J. C. Russell, *Dictionary of writers of thirteenth-century England* (1936). The 1906 catalogue reads, incorrectly, 'Chesard [? Thesard]'.

137 The title 'Sequax magistri' is written in a fifteenth-century hand on the outside of the second cover of MS. F. 54.

161 Young's title is identical with that given to MS. F. 139 in the 1697 catalogue and in MS. Tanner 268.

163 The title on the medieval label, now pasted to a flyleaf of MS. F. 39, is 'Questionista'. As usual it is copied in MS. Tanner 268.

167 This manuscript was Q. 38 in the 1697 catalogue. It is now bound up in Harley 4967 with another manuscript, also from Worcester, which is entered as Q. 80 in the 1697 catalogue, but is not described by Young.

174 Young was not interested in the legal manuscripts and some of his entries are difficult to identify. It is probable that the label of MS. F. 110 read, quite wrongly, 'Liber decretalium', since that is the title given in MS. Tanner

[1] In one manuscript, Laud misc. 176 (s. xiv), the meaning of the name Promatheus is explained in a passage near the end of the section 'ante genesim' (f. 49ᵛ): 'Demostenis pro thesifonte, id est librum quod demostenes rethor scripsit ad defensionem thesifontis, et ideo dicitur iste liber pro thesifonte, id est pro eo factus; sicut iste liber dicitur promatheus, id est pro matheo factus. Cum enim legere[m] matheum decreui utile fore libri illius uocabula nouiciis exponere. Hoc opus agressus sum ut non solum mathei sed etiam omnium librorum biblie uocabulorum significata illis elucesserent, unde et a principali libro nomen imposui'. This passage, from *sicut iste liber*, is lacking in the Worcester manuscript and in Magdalen College MS. lat. 112.

268. In the 1697 catalogue it appears as 'Textus decretalium'. The label itself is *in situ*, but is illegible. The manuscript contains part of Justinian's Codex.

182   There is no title inside MS. F. 12, but 'Huguo super decret'' is written on the backstrip of the medieval binding. The erroneous title in all the catalogues is perhaps traceable to the medieval label, only the mark of which remains on the second cover. For the work of Huguitio see Kuttner, *Repertorium der Kanonistik* (1937), p. 157.

183   This manuscript was at Worcester in the second half of the seventeenth century and is F. 60 in MS. Tanner 268, 'Leges et decreta Gratiani'.

195   The title in MS. F. 62 is 'Summa confessorum compilata a fratre Johanne lectoris fratrum predicatorum'.

203   The inscription on the medieval label of MS. F. 73 is 'Porphyrius super 5 uniuersalia predicamenta et libros posteriorum. sophestria secundum usum oxonie. Quidam (*sic*) questiones de quantitate et motu et aliis'. This is reproduced almost exactly in MS. Tanner 268 and with slight variations in the 1697 catalogue and by Young.

214   The name written on the second cover of Q. 43 is given as Newnam in the 1697 catalogue and as Newman in MS. Tanner 268. Only 'New' is now legible.

215   The titles given to Q. 70 by Young, in MS. Tanner 268, and in the 1697 catalogue are derived evidently from the medieval label on the second cover, only the mark of which now remains.

216   For the identification with MS. Hatton 48 see N. R. Ker, 'The provenance of the oldest manuscript of the Rule of St Benedict', *Bodleian Library Record*, II (1941), 28. To the account there given should be added the fact that the name 'Thomas bryne' which occurs on f. 9 (s. xv/xvi) is found also in the form 'byrne thomas' on the second leaf of Register 1 (MS. A. 4) at Worcester.

218   Royal MS. 15 B. iv is entered as Q. 26, 'Leges Baelwardi', in MS. Tanner 268 and as Q. 25 in the 1697 catalogue. The 'Leges Eadwardi Regis', which seems to have been adopted, in a mangled form, as the short title of the whole volume (it was evidently inscribed on the old label), is now missing: it came between ff. 145 and 146, according to the old table of contents.

225   The title of the last item on the old label of MS. F. 38 is 'Libri decretalium una cum decretis' and this is reproduced nearly in MS. Tanner 268.

227   In the medieval table of contents of MS. F. 3 (f. 259ᵛ) 'Kykeley' is given as the author of 'questiones' beginning on f. 62: the table is in the main hand of the manuscript, but the name 'Kykeley' is probably in another hand. Cf. Pelster in *Misc. Fr. Ehrle*, I (1924), 324.

228   The 'Summa matrimonii', with *incipit* 'Quoniam frequenter in foro', begins on f. 100 of MS. Q. 98.

232   Young's title for the second item in MS. F. 116 is derived from the *explicit* on f. 48, 'Expliciunt proporciones bone et utiles'. The last words are blurred and hard to read: we owe the solution of them to Mr R. A. B. Mynors. The title in MS. Tanner 268 and in the 1697 catalogue is 'Sophismata Hartilbury cum Consequentiis. Mag. Richardi Ferbrygg (*1697* de Ferrybrigge)'.

233   'Textus super logica Aristotelis' was probably written on the medieval label of this manuscript, if, as seems likely, the entry of these words in MS. Tanner 268 as the description of F. 66 refers to the present MS. F. 165.

240 The initial letter of the first text in MS. Hatton 11 (*S.C.* 4132) contains the name 'Johannes de Clyva monachus'. This is John Clive, sacrist and precentor at Worcester in the early fifteenth century. His account-rolls, preserved at Worcester, are written in the same hand as MS. Hatton 11.

242 Young's information about the 'Prophetiæ Hernerici' was derived, no doubt, from the old label, only the mark of which now remains on the second cover of MS. Q. 15. The prophecy is common and begins usually 'Lilium regnans'.

253 The editors of the *Catalogue of Royal and King's Manuscripts in the British Museum* consider that Royal MS. 5 F. iii is 'written in several hands, more or less of Mercian type'. What appears to be the backstrip of the medieval binding of MS. 5 F. iii is preserved at the beginning of Royal MS. 5 E. iv.

264 The old label of MS. F. 35, now pasted to the foot of f. 2, reads 'Wynesched (*or* Wyuesched) de motu locali et aliis'.

265 MS. Q. 90 does not seem to be imperfect, although the bottoms of some of the leaves have been damaged.

269 MS. Q. 81 begins 'Expediuimus nos', before which the word 'postquam' has been inserted.

275 For the 'De modo medendi' see Lynn Thorndike, *Incipits of mediaeval scientific writings in Latin* (1937), col. 152.

293 This manuscript contained, according to the descriptions in the 1697 catalogue and in MS. Tanner 268, not only the *Lapidarius* and Nequam, *De utensilibus*, but also Horace, *De arte poetica*, the *Græcismus* and other texts. The description in MS. Tanner 268 ends with the words 'Liber Perley'.

294 Young's account suggests that leaves have been lost from MS. F. 137 in recent times. The other copy to which he refers is his no. 289 = MS. F. 99.

296 This is the *incipit* of Nequam, *De utensilibus*.

304 The description of MS. F. 118 in MS. Tanner 268, 'Sophestria secundum usum Oxoniæ. Item tractatus de quantitate qualitate et insolubilitate et aliis logicalibus et sophistrialibus', is derived, no doubt, from the medieval label, now lost. The manuscript contains texts 'de quantitate', but there does not seem to be any obvious reason for ascribing them to Milverley. 'In nomine trino...incipio quod Mylverle' is written at the head of f. 113.

305 Royal MS. 15 A. xxxiii contains an early ex-libris inscription of the monastery of St Remi at Reims, 'Liber sancti Remigii studio Gifardi'.

306 The descriptions of MS. F. 119 in MS. Tanner 268 and in the 1697 catalogue, 'Tractatus de Syllogismis et eorum differentiis, de Prædicamentis, Sophisticis Elenchis, de Priore et Posteriore', are derived, no doubt, from the medieval label, now lost.

309 Young's title is unfortunately vague. It seems very likely that the manuscript referred to is Royal MS. 2 A. xx. The editors of the *Catalogue of Royal and King's Manuscripts* say of this famous prayer-book that 'the nature of the ornament and various liturgical points show so much Celtic influence as to make it probable that it was written in Mercia or Northumbria, while added collects prove it to have belonged in the tenth or eleventh century to some Benedictine monastery'. The tenth-century Old English glosses are certainly Mercian, not Northumbrian. The manuscript belonged in 1649 to John Theyer, whose other ancient manuscripts were procured from Worcester.

310 'Wehoedale' is perhaps the actual reading of the badly faded medieval label now attached to the first pastedown of MS. Q. 54.

324 MS. Hatton 6 (*S.C.* 4129) is a handsome book with wide empty margins, s. xii/xiii. There is a very obvious gap after f. 102, where 26 leaves are missing. A label pasted to the second cover of the medieval binding bears the title 'Canones apostolorum'.

330 The names Thomas Grene, Webley, and Thomas Grymley (s. xv/xvi) and the note 'Thomas Wlstanus hunc libellum perlegit anno domini 1520' occur in Royal MS. 8 D. xiii. Worcester Obedientiary Rolls show that in 1521 Grene was coquinarius and that Grymley then celebrated his first mass. Humphrey Webley, a monk before the Dissolution, afterwards became prebendary of the ninth stall. For Grene see also the note on Young, no. 98.

333 Royal MS. 5 E. xiii contains the fourteenth-century pressmark $\dfrac{R}{\text{CXCII}}$ altered to $\dfrac{R}{\text{XXVII}}$.

337 This version of Æsop has been edited by Georg Thiele, *Der lateinische Æsop des Romulus* (1910).

341 Young's title 'tractatus de officiis anni' refers to the text on ff. 63–72 of MS. Q. 78, beginning 'Queritur quare quadragesima celebratur'. The manuscript is not in the 1697 catalogue. It is Q. 38 in MS. Tanner 268, 'Sermones poenitentiarum. Tractatus de officiis anni'. These titles are derived, no doubt, from the medieval label, now lost.

342 Eton College MS. 96 contains no evidence that it is a Worcester book. It is, however, the only one of the many manuscripts of the *Compendium* of Peter of Poitiers which agrees with Young's description of no. 342 (see P. S. Moore, *The works of Peter of Poitiers*, 1936). The manuscript measures $18\frac{1}{2} \times 13\frac{3}{4}$ inches. It begins 'Incipit compendium ueteris testamenti editum a magistro petro pictauiensi et cancellario parisiensi. Considerans ystorie prolixitatem.' The Compendium proper is followed by a brief general history, with special attention to England, ending at the year 1241 with a note on the Tartar invasions. The manuscript is not included in Bernard's list of the Eton library (1697). The names 'Elizabeth Flovern' on f. 9 (M. R. James read Flobern) and 'William Hardine' (?) on f. 25 appear to be of the seventeenth century. The binding is modern.

p. 60. Young refers to the following manuscripts formerly belonging to Thomas Allen: Martianus Capella in Paris, Bibliothèque Nationale, lat. 8802; Sidonius Apollinaris in Bodleian, Digby 61; Sallust in Digby 42; Symeon of Durham's history, formerly ascribed to Turgot, in British Museum, Cotton Faustina A. v; the cartulary of St Frideswide, Oxford, in Corpus Christi College, Oxford, 160; Robert Talbot's commentary on the Antonine itinerary, 'quoad Britanniam', in Bodleian, e Mus. 199 (*S.C.* 3709).

p. 60. For Grafton House see above, p. 2. Two manuscripts of Richard (*not* William) Barre's work on the Bible are Lambeth Palace 105 ff. 1–112 and Harley 3255. The former is from Bury St Edmunds. Barre was Archdeacon of Ely 'about 1191 and 1196' according to Le Neve.

APPENDICES

I

MEDIEVAL LABELS ON WORCESTER MANUSCRIPTS

T HE want of a medieval catalogue is partly supplied by the inscriptions on the labels which are still attached to many of the books. This labelling is the only notable piece of librarianship at Worcester in the Middle Ages of which we have record. Late in the fifteenth century a label seems to have been pasted on the outside of the second cover of every book in the library.[1] The label was simply pasted on, not secured by nails nor covered by horn. The inscriptions on the labels are in several hands, one of which has a humanist character. They are full, not to say verbose. Sometimes they are wildly incorrect. They are of value because they provide definite evidence that books now in the Cathedral Library were at Worcester in the late Middle Ages, because they provide a means of identifying Worcester books which have strayed from the library, and because they are the source of nearly all the descriptions in MS. Tanner 268, of many of the descriptions in the 1697 catalogue and of some of the titles in the 1906 catalogue, usually at second-hand, e.g. those of F. 65, F. 67, Q. 11 (misread), Q. 26, Q. 31, Q. 71. Young refers sometimes to the labels, but he did not usually base his descriptions on them.

The following manuscripts at Worcester retain their labels, either *in situ*, or removed to a flyleaf or to one of the pastedowns: F. 1, 4, 5, 6, 7, 11, 19, 21, 23, 24, 29, 35, 38, 39, 41, 42, 44, 48, 50, 51, 54, 55, 56, 57, 60, 62, 64, 65, 67, 71, 72, 73, 78, 79,[2] 81, 82, 86, 87, 88, 91, 96, 98, 100, 101, 104, 105, 106, 108, 110, 111, 112, 115, 117, 125, 127, 128, 132, 133, 135, 136, 137, 138, 140, 145, 151, 152, 153, 154, 164, 170; Q. 1, 2,[2] 3, 4, 5, 11, 13, 14, 16, 22, 24,[2] 26, 27, 29, 30, 31, 34, 44, 46, 47, 48, 50, 51, 53, 54, 55, 59, 62, 64, 65, 66, 69, 71, 72, 76,[3] 82, 85, 92, 94.

Some of these labels are fragmentary and some of them are illegible, wholly or in part, but the original readings can often be recovered with the help of MS. Tanner 268.

The label has disappeared from the following manuscripts, but the mark of it remains on the second cover: F. 12, 13, 14, 33,[4] 36 (?), 49,[4] 52, 69 (?), 83, 97,[4] 107,[4] 116,[4] 123, 139 (?), 143, 147 (?), 155; Q. 7, 9, 15, 17, 20 (?), 28, 37, 66,[4] 70, 88.[4]

---

[1] In MS. Q. 5 the label is on the first cover: there is a facsimile of it in the 1906 catalogue, opposite p. xvi.

[2] All that remains of the labels of F. 79, Q. 2, Q. 24 is now stuck on to the fore-edge of a leaf in the middle of the manuscript (cf. the note in the 1906 catalogue on F. 39, the label of which was formerly in this position).

[3] Q. 76 has been rebound, but the old cover, to which a fragment of the label is attached, is kept in the library as Add. MS. 46.

[4] F. 33, 49, 97, 107, 116, Q. 66, 88 have been rebound, but the old covers have been preserved.

In the Bodleian library, MSS. Auct. F. 1. 9,[1] Auct. F. 5. 16,[1] Auct. F. inf. 1. 3, Bodley 81,[1] 633, 868, Hatton 6, Hatton 23 (*S.C.* Nos. 4137, 2581, 2747, 2269, 1966, 2749, 4129, 4115) retain their labels *in situ*, or removed to a flyleaf or to one of the pastedowns. The mark of the label remains on the second cover of MS. Hatton 11 and possibly on that of MS. Hatton 48 (*S.C.* Nos. 4132, 4118).

The editors of the *Catalogue of Royal and King's Manuscripts in the British Museum* refer to labels pasted inside Royal MSS. 2 C. vii and 2 E. vi, both Worcester books. There is a label on the MS. now at Aberystwyth: see below, p. 79.

II

WORCESTER MS. F. 163

OF the accessions since 1622–3 by far the most important is F. 163, a handsome psalter with the commentary of Gilbert de la Porrée, written about A.D. 1200, which is entered in the Book of Donations to the Library amongst other books given in 1675 by Dr William Thomas, then dean of Worcester. It is there described as 'M:Scr: pergamen: in Psalmos'. There is a fifteenth-century inscription on a flyleaf of the manuscript, 'Dominus tomas traueis aliquando plowmakar' and another, in a sixteenth-century hand, 'verus est Ashelok possessor codicis hujus, te rogat ut reddas si reperiri datur', and at the end are scribbles of Welsh names, 'Lewis Johnes, Bett (?), Lewis Johnes of the Pont (?)'. The arms of the See, which at that time were used by the dean and Chapter also, are stamped on the fore-edge, as they are on other books given in 1675 by Thomas, Edward Reynolds, and Barnabas Oley.[2]

The chief interest of the volume lies in the six leaves of a manuscript of St Gregory's 'Regula Pastoralis', written in England in the eighth century, which were used to strengthen the medieval binding. These leaves, which were formerly pasted down in more than one thickness on the boards, were removed about 1912 under the instructions of Canon J. M. Wilson, then librarian, and bound together. They are now kept separately as Addit. MS. 3. They are described by E. A. Lowe, *Codices Latini Antiquiores*, II (1935), no. 264, and described and reproduced in facsimile by C. H. Turner, *Early Worcester MSS.*, 1916, pp. xviii–xxiv, and 15–26. Turner assumed that they came from one of the ancient books of the church of Worcester and that they 'may well have been written at Worcester itself', but there is unfortunately no proof at present that the manuscript, in the binding of which they have been preserved, was at Worcester before 1675. The leaves were no doubt used in binding before the sixteenth century, at which time F. 163 appears to have been in secular hands, perhaps in Wales, or on the border of Wales. It is worth noting that Dr Thomas, who gave the book, was a Welshman, and had numerous con-

---

[1] Auct. F. 1. 9, Auct. F. 5. 16 and Bodley 81 have been identified as Worcester books solely on the evidence of the labels and the hands in which the inscriptions are written.

[2] A 'Brasse-stampe of the Colledge Armes' had been bought in 1667. In May 1675 1ˢ· 6ᵈ· was paid 'for stamping the Church Arms on Dʳ Jackson's works'. [Treasurer's Accounts.]

nections with Wales. Born in 1613, he was educated at Caermarthen and St John's College, Oxford, and later at Jesus College, where he was made fellow in 1635. Returning to Wales he held various livings until 1644 when he was deprived. At the Restoration he became precentor of St David's, and in 1665 dean of Worcester, retaining this office after he was made bishop of St David's in 1677. From 1683 to 1689, when he died, he was bishop of Worcester.

III

MANUSCRIPTS IN TANNER 268 CATALOGUE (c. 1676) NOT FOUND IN 1697 CATALOGUE

An asterisk denotes that the volume is no longer at Worcester

			Young	Now
1*	F. 60	Leges et decreta Gratiani	183	—
2*	F. 62	Vocabularius	—	—
3	F. 104	Quinque libri Innocentii papae IIII super Decretales	177	F. 170
4*	F. 124	Liber de sacramentis	—	—
5*	F. 127	S. Thomas in 4 lib. Sententiarum	—	—
6	Q. 5	Expositio super Lucam	66	Q. 82
7	Q. 16	Thomas super 4tum lib. Sententiarum	134	Q. 88
8	Q. 18	Quæstiones super Metaphysicam	265	Q. 90
9*	Q. 27	Gerardinus de floribus dietarum	275	—
10	Q. 38	Sermones pænitentiarum	341	Q. 78
11*	Q. 67	Precationes in festis sanctorum, etc.	252	—
12	Q. 68	Summa Reymundi	228	Q. 98

IV

QUARTO MANUSCRIPTS LISTED IN 1697 AND NO LONGER AT WORCESTER

The titles given in the 1697 catalogue have been abbreviated here: they are quoted in full in the 1906 catalogue, pp. 173–5

18	Prælectiones P. Maximiliani, S. J., 1576	Replaced by	Collationes (? Y. 312)
25	Vita Modwennæ, etc. (Y. 218: now B.M., Royal 15 B. iv)	„	Vocabularium theologicum (Y. 190)
32	Liber Hymnorum cum notis musicis	„	A collection of Fragments
38	Prometheus de contrarietate Canonum, etc. (Y. 167: now part of B.M., Harley 4967)	„	'Questiones W. de Burley' (Y. 226)
57	Vita Barlaam, etc. (Y. 286: now B.M., Harley 5394)	„	Sermones G. de Tornaco (Y. 239)

58   Lapidarius, etc. (Y. 293)   Replaced by 'Note super libr. pri-
                                                           orum' (Y. 313)
     ⸢Varii tractatus in Theologia   „   'Magister ceremoni-
73   ⸤Commentarius in Apocalypsim   arum'
      idiomate Anglicano
78   Sermo anglice, etc.   „   Sermones (Y. 341)
80   Hymni Ecclesiastici, etc. (now part   „   Parabole   Salomonis,
     of B.M., Harley 4967)   etc.
81   Manuscriptus Codex Sinensis   „   'Collectio secunda libri
                                                          sufficientie' (Y. 269)

V

MANUSCRIPTS ADDED SINCE 1623

FOLIOS

		DONOR	DATE OF GIFT
148	Bedæ opera quædam		Listed in 1697
158[1]	Psalterium Latine et Anglice	William Swift	c. 1685
161[2]	Missale ad usum eccles. Hereford-ensis		Listed in 1697
162	Biblia Sacra		Listed in 1697
163[3]	Psalterium cum commentario	Dr William Thomas	1675
166[4]	Psalterium Latine et Anglice *paper*	William Swift	c. 1685
171	Augustinus de civitate Dei	Anthony Bidolph of Ledbury (1658–1718)	c. 1698
172[5]	Passio Nichodemi		early 18th century

[1] The Book of Donations, in which are entered 'the names of the Benefactors contributing towards Furnishing the Library A° Dⁿⁱ 1675 —', records that 'William Swift Esq.' gave to the library the two manuscripts now F. 158 and F. 166, and a third entitled 'A Manuscript Collection of English Translations in verse. Quarto'. This last is no longer in the library. Swift was a Worcester citizen.

[2] On the last leaf is 'Sir John Child, 1742'. The title written in an eighteenth-century hand at the head of the manuscript is identical with the title in the 1697 catalogue: 'Missale vetus ad usum Sarum, eleganter admodum descriptum et exornatum'.

[3] See p. 70 for a further note on this manuscript.

[4] On the first flyleaf are the names 'Thomas Jefferis, 1648, his book, William Jefferis, Lennard Jefferis, 1648. Three other manuscripts bear the name Jefferies, F. 70, F. 128 and F. 158. Of these the first has 'W. Jefferies, the second, 'William Jeffreis' and the third, 'Leonard Jefferys'. The connection of the Jefferies family with Worcester manuscripts is obscure. F. 158 and F. 166 reached the library c. 1685. F. 70, on the other hand, is listed by Young (no. 277) and F. 128, which is also listed by him (no. 62), contains a medieval Worcester ex-libris inscription. For the pedigree of the Jefferies family see Nash, *Collections for the History of Worcestershire* (1781–2), I, 267–8. See also note 1.

[5] The manuscript contains the name 'William Ballard' with the date 1707, and the signature of Dr William Thomas, the Worcester antiquary (1670–1738), grandson of Dean Thomas and the author of *A Survey of the Cathedral Church of Worcester* (1737).

QUARTOS

36[1]	Carte et statuta regni Anglie	Listed in MS. Tanner 268 *c.* 1676
68[2]	Summa Theologie	Listed in 1697
73	'Magister ceremoniarum'	
75[3]	Hugo de S. Victore de Arca Noe	Listed in 1697
79[4]	Galfridi de Vino Salvo Poetria nova	Listed in 1697
80	Parabole Salomonis, etc., glo.	Dr William Burrell, 1765 Chancellor of Worcester
83[5]	Biblia Latina	
84[2]	New Testament in English	Listed in 1697
86[6]	Breviarium secundum usum ecclesie Herefordensis	
91[7]	Materie historiales Biblie	early 18th century
95[8]	Controversiae nostri temporis (Robert Parsons)	early 18th century

VI

THE LIST OF QUARTO MANUSCRIPTS 82–104 ADDED IN PENCIL AT THE END OF THE 1781 CATALOGUE[9]

		YOUNG	1906
82	Beda in Lucam	66	Q. 82
83	Biblia	—	83
84	Computus Thomæ Prioris (a Roll)[10]	—	—
85	Tractatus de diversis materiis etc. The cover is a Roll of the Bishop of Worcester's expences[11]	246	85

[1] At one time in the possession of Francis Harewell of Birlingham (d. *c.* 1635). A Thomas Harewell gave books to the library *c.* 1690.

[2] Formerly belonged to John Prideaux, bishop of Worcester 1641–50.

[3] From the Franciscan convent at Shrewsbury. On f. 1 is the inscription 'ex D. H. P. ecclesie Wigorn. Sacrum'.

[4] On f. 188 is the inscription in a sixteenth/seventeenth-century hand 'to my lovinge frinde William Elly at Solwarpe'. A William Ellie, Yeoman, died at Salwarpe in 1617 (E. A. Fry, *Worcester Wills*, Worc. Hist. Society, 1910, II, 82).

[5] The initials A.S. are stamped on the binding.

[6] The calendar contains obits of the Brugge family.

[7] In Dr William Thomas's possession in 1733. See p. 72, note 5.

[8] Has note in Dr William Thomas's hand.

[9] See above, p. 29.

[10] Perhaps one of the three Rolls of Thomas Musard, 1456–69 (Cath. Mun. C. 400–2).

[11] Q. 85 has been rebound and the cover is now missing.

		YOUNG	1906
86	Lectionale	—	Q. 86
87	Festivale	327	87
88	Liber quartus Sententiarum	134	88
89	In Joh'is Evangelium	68	94
90	Sententiae super Metha*physicam*	265	90
91	Collectio secunda libri sufficientiæ a princi-piis Physicæ	269	81
92	Sermones	—	—
93	Magister Ceremoniarum etc.	—	73
94	Materiæ Historiales Bibliæ	—	91
95	Person's Controversiæ nostri temporis in epi-tomen redactæ 1583	—	95
96	Parabole Salomonis	—	80
97	De legibus canonicis[1]	—	—
98	Walteri De Burley Quæstiones	226	38
99	Sermones	—	—
100	Tractatus	—	—
101	Tractatus	—	—
102	Summa Penitentiæ	228	98
103	[blank]		
104	[blank]		

[1] No longer in the library.

VII
CONCORDANCE OF 1906 CATALOGUE AND YOUNG'S CATALOGUE

Some of the identifications, although not marked with a query, are inevitably doubtful: see above, p. 7

FOLIOS

1906	Young	1906	Young	1906	Young	1906	Young
F. 1	92	F. 46	Mag. Sent.	F. 91	87	F. 136	171
2	245	47	86	92	97	137	294
3	227	48	249	93	27	138	258
4	266	49	69	94	77	139	161
5	101	50	153	95†	82	140	127
6	118	51	49	96	261	141	184
7	186	52	63	97	? 175	142	1
8	Mag. Sent.	53	Mag. Sent.	98	Mag. Sent.	143	78
9	71	54	137	99	289	144	185
10	107	55	14	100	180	145	268
11	15	56	151	101	142	146	191
12	182	57	50	102	141	147	271
13	284	58	*	103	143	148	‡
14	169	59	187	104	140	149	30
15	201	60	224	105	144	150	188
16	109	61	96	106	146	151	198
17	199	62	195	107	136	152	44
18	255	63	260	108	138	153	48
19	241	64	150	109	139	154	285
20	208	65	295	110	? 174	155	85
21	72	66	234	111	206	156	202
22	283	67	64	112	251	157	300
23	254	68	262	113	193	158	‡
24	170	69	149	114	76	159	181
25	7	70	277	115	236	160	? 57
26	10	71	80	116	232	161	‡
27	9	72	308	117	250	162	‡
28	8	73	203	118	304	163	‡
29	*	74	168	119	306	164	160
30	323	75	52	120	204	165	233
31	152	76	11	121	108	166	‡
32	29	77	105	122	211	167	145
33	88, 91 or 93	78	166	123	290	168	? 209
34	95	79	157	124	126	169	267
35	264	80	307	125	207	170	177
36	100	81	4	126	99	171	‡
37	88, 91 or 93	82	2	127	194	172	‡
38	225	83	47	128	62	173	*
39	163	84	51	129	197	174	§
40	270	85	272	130	94	175	210
41	34	86	256	131	178	176	154
42	259	87	200	132	32	177	? 212
43	106	88	Mag. Sent.	133	116		
44	159	89	84	134	Mag. Sent.		
45	247	90	179	135	173		

* Ancient Worcester manuscript not identifiable in Young's catalogue.
† F. 95 = Q. 93; see above, p. 28, note 4. ‡ Added since 1622–3.
§ Fragments of Ælfric's Grammar. See p. 19, note 2.

QUARTOS

1906	YOUNG	1906	YOUNG	1906	YOUNG	1906	YOUNG
Q. 1	219	26	302	Q. 51	43	Q. 76	46
2	83	27	340	52	280	77	117
3	325	28	89	53	220	78	341
4	331	29	338	54	310	79	†
5	229	30	230	55	326	80	†
6	113	31	164	56	115	81	269
7	42	32	*	57	239	82	66
8	58	33	155	58	313	83	†
9	120	34	263	59	332	84	†
10	75	35	135	60	279	85	246
11	111	36	†	61	122	86	†
12	121	37	288	62	196	87	327
13	231	38	226	63	329	88	134
14	244	39	281	64	237	89	299
15	242	40	273	65	112	90	265
16	65	41	276	66	336	91	†
17	328	42	165	67	123	92	311
18	? 312	43	214	68	†	93	82
19	125	44	90	69	148	94	68
20	156	45	114	70	215	95	†
21	40	46	334	71	162	96	274
22	243	47	Mag. Sent.	72	287	97	303
23	238	48	45	73	†	98	228
24	31	49	278	74	335	99	? 315
25	190	50	124	75	†	100	? 314

* Ancient Worcester manuscript not identifiable in Young's catalogue.
† Added since 1622–3.

VIII

THE 'OFFA' BIBLE AND THE NERO-MIDDLETON CARTULARY

OF a great early-eighth-century Bible eleven leaves and fragments of a twelfth leaf are extant. Ten complete leaves were used as endleaves and covers to sixteenth-century cartularies of the Willoughby family estates bound in the reign of Edward VI, and fragments of another leaf were cut into strips to strengthen the binding of one of the cartularies. These leaves were found by Mr W. H. Stevenson when he was cataloguing the manuscripts of Lord Middleton at Wollaton Hall, near Nottingham.[1] They were sold by Lord Middleton to the British Museum in 1937 and now form Additional MS. 45025. Another leaf was bought by Canon Greenwell of Durham from a Newcastle bookseller about 1890. It had been in use as the cover of an account book of *c.* 1780 and is now British Museum Additional MS. 37777.[2]

It was seen at once that these leaves came from a sister manuscript to the Codex Amiatinus at Florence, which is both one of the most important copies of the Vulgate in existence and one of the largest books of the early Middle Ages. As an inscription shows, the Amiatinus is to be identified with one of the 'tres pandectes novæ translationis' which, Bede tells us, were written at the direction of Ceolfrid, abbot of Jarrow and Monkwearmouth (d. 716).[3] The Amiatinus itself was designed as a gift to St Peter's, Rome: of the other two copies one was for Jarrow and the other for Monkwearmouth. The leaves now at the British Museum are the meagre remains of one of these copies. Like the Amiatinus they are written in a distinct type of uncial of about the year 700, in double columns of 44 lines, but the width and height of each column are usually slightly less than in the Amiatinus and the general effect of the script and lay-out is rather less stately.

Both Bibles have been described by E. A. Lowe, *Codices Latini Antiquiores*, pt. 2 (1935), no. 177 (Brit. Mus.) and pt. 3 (1938), no. 299 (Amiatinus). Lowe gives facsimiles and full bibliographies and has shown conclusively that the uncial was written by English scribes (see especially *C.L.A.* pt. 2, p. xvi). Reduced facsimiles of two leaves of Brit. Mus. Add. MS. 45025 are in *Friends of the National Libraries, Annual Report* 1937–8, pls. II, III, and of one leaf in *British Museum Quarterly*, xii (1938), pl. xiv (accompanying description by Idris Bell on p. 39) showing, much reduced, the complete page beginning 'filii usque' and ending 'viginti annis'.

---

[1] W. H. Stevenson, *Report on the manuscripts of Lord Middleton at Wollaton Hall* (Hist. MSS. Comm.), 1911, p. 196. The manuscripts are now at Birdsall House, near Malton.

[2] The clearest evidence that the Greenwell leaf and the Middleton leaves come from the same manuscript is afforded by paragraph-marks which occur in both fragments and appear to be the work of the early-fourteenth-century scribe who wrote 'Explicit Regum liber tertius. Incipit quartus' at the head of one of the Middleton leaves.

[3] Beda, *Historia abbatum*, ed. C. Plummer, *Baedae opera historica* (1896), I, 379.

Stevenson found among Lord Middleton's manuscripts not only the Bible leaves, but also a leaf and strips of another leaf of an eleventh-century Worcester cartulary, which had been used in binding a 'colpyt booke' for the year 1548. This discovery suggested the possibility that the Bible leaves also might come from Worcester, and both Stevenson and C. H. Turner thought it not unlikely that they had once formed part of the Bible known to have been given to Worcester by King Offa.[1] The cartulary leaf and strips were seen to come from the same manuscript as four leaves now in the Cotton collection (Cotton MS. Nero E. i, pt. 2, ff. 181–4), which, as appears from scribbles on the first leaf, had been used formerly in binding a 'booke of acountes'.

The theory of the Worcester provenance of the Bible leaves remained a theory, unsupported by real evidence, until 1940, when Sir Ivor Atkins suggested that the Nero-Middleton cartulary leaves 'were originally inserted in the Bible'.[2] He drew attention to the unusual format of the cartulary leaves, to their date, mid-eleventh century, rather than 'about the year 1000', as Stevenson had thought, and to the important passage in Hemming which records that St Wulstan ordered copies of Worcester charters to be written in the Bible of the Church ('in bibliotheca sancte ecclesie scribi').[3] The large-folio size of the leaves and their arrangement in double columns are certainly very curious for an eleventh-century English manuscript and indeed for any manuscript written in England between c. 800 and c. 1100.[4] On palaeographical grounds the date can hardly be earlier than the middle of the eleventh century and is probably somewhat later: at any rate it falls within the period of St Wulstan's rule as prior and bishop of Worcester (c. 1055–95).

Sir Ivor Atkins pointed out that the cartulary leaves and the Bible fragments 'are about the same size', but it is worth giving more exact details. Both Bible and cartulary are in double columns of 44 lines with double bounding lines enclosing each column. The writing-area of the Bible is given as 360 × 255 mm. by Lowe, who appears to have measured the width from the outer bounding line on the left of the first column to the outer bounding line on the right of the second column. The writing-area of the cartulary is about 356 × 253 mm., the width being measured in the same way, but the columns are slightly broader than those of the Bible, the space between them being only 23 mm., as against 28 mm. in the Bible. This correspondence in size is remarkable and seems to us to provide very strong evidence that the cartulary was formerly bound up with the Bible.[5]

The Nero-Middleton cartulary is at least thirty to forty years later in date than the cartulary which forms the first part of Cotton Tiberius A. xiii. The whole of Tiberius A. xiii is always called 'Hemming's cartulary', but the first part of it (ff. 1–118), except for some of the additions in spaces originally blank,

[1] Stevenson, op. cit., p. 196; C. H. Turner, Early Worcester MSS. (1916), p. xlii.
[2] Antiquaries Journal, xx (1940), 221.
[3] Hemingi Chartularium, op. cit., p. 285.
[4] The margins of Nero E. i have been drastically cut, so that the leaves measure now only about 16 × 11·2 inches, but the Middleton leaf is still as much as 17½ inches in height.
[5] It should be noted that the height of each column in the reproduction of the Bible (Add. 37777) in New Pal. Soc. is 370 mm., not, as Lowe says, 360 mm. The manuscript itself is not available at present. Lowe's plate in Codd. Lat. Antiq. is slightly less than actual size.

was written three quarters of a century or more before Hemming's time, and Hemming's only possible connection with this part is that he may have been responsible for combining it with his own work beginning on f. 119. The relation of Nero-Middleton to Tiberius needs investigation. Roughly speaking, the charters in the former are copied in the same order as those in the latter, but in an abbreviated version, the scribe being concerned apparently to get as much as possible into the space at his disposal. Calculations are hazardous, but if, as seems not unlikely, the Nero-Middleton cartulary contained almost exactly the same collection of material as Tiberius ff. 1–114, but excluding, probably, some of the miscellaneous additions in the latter, the whole of it may have been fitted into about 24 leaves or 3 quires. This amount could have been added to the thousand leaves of the great Bible[1] without making any appreciable difference to its bulk.

IX

WORCESTER MANUSCRIPTS NOT DESCRIBED BY YOUNG

SIXTY manuscripts which belonged, certainly or very probably, to the medieval library at Worcester are not described by Young.[2] Four of them remain at Worcester (see above, p. 7, note 1). Nearly all the others are known to have been alienated before 1622, but it is possible that a few escaped Young's attention and remained in the Cathedral Library until a later date. Forty out of the fifty-six are noticed above, pp. 7–13, and forty-three are described by Turner, *Early Worcester MSS.* (1916), Appendix IV, Anglo-Saxon MSS. nos. 1, 7–9, 11, 13–17, Latin MSS. nos. 1–7, 15–19, 19*, 20–28, 32, 33, 40, 41, 43–46, 48–50.[3] The following thirteen manuscripts are not described by Turner:

1   Aberystwyth, National Library of Wales, Peniarth MS. 386, s. xiii. The inscription, 'Liber sancte marie Wigornie', is in a fifteenth-century hand. The medieval binding bears a label *in situ*, inscribed (s. xv) 'Vita sanctissimi patris nostri Wolstani cum miraculis in metris. Biblia tota a magistro petro riga metrice edita'. The book was 'Donum Magistri Moreye Junii 24 1602' to an unknown recipient. It is described by Dr Robin Flower in *National Library of Wales Journal*, 1 (1939–40), 119–30.

2   Cambridge, Univ. Libr., Kk. 4. 6, s. xii in., a great collection of texts— *inter alia* the *Liber Pontificalis*—the compilation of which has been ascribed to William of Malmesbury,[4] but is more certainly connected with the work of John of Worcester, the early-twelfth-century editor of the chronicle of Florence. Some of the writing is in a hand, probably John's, which occurs also in the Worcester manuscripts now Corpus Christi College, Oxford, 157 and Bodleian, Auct. F. 1. 9.

3   Gloucester, Dean and Chapter Library, medical and scientific texts, *c.* 1200, 'Liber fratris Thome Mor' monachi monasterii Wygorn'' in the fifteenth

---

[1] The Codex Amiatinus contains 1030 leaves.

[2] This number does not include fragments of manuscripts consisting of twenty leaves, or less.

[3] Turner, nos. 13, 14 are not from Worcester, but from Rochester. For other rejected Worcester ascriptions see Ker, *Medieval Libraries*, p. 117.

[4] M. R. James, *Two ancient English scholars*, 1931, p. 20.

century. The manuscript is described in *Hist. MSS. Comm.*, 12th Report, pt. ix, p. 398. More held various offices in the monastery from 1393 to 1410.

4   London, British Museum, Add. 25031, a medical miscellany, s. xiii, the binding leaves of which come from the same motet-book as leaves in Bodleian, lat. liturg. d. 20 (taken from the bindings of the Worcester manuscripts now Bodleian, Auct. F. inf. 1. 3 and Bodley 862) and in Worcester Cath., Add. MS. 68 (taken from the bindings of the cathedral manuscripts F. 34, F. 125 and F. 133). The name 'musard' is on f. 5 (cf. 'Johannes Musard'[1] in Worcester Cath., MSS. F. 90 and F. 93), and there are other connections with Worcester. The manuscript was acquired by the Museum at the Tenison sale, 1 July, 1861, lot 86. For the motet-book see Dom Anselm Hughes, *Worcester Mediæval Harmony*, Plainsong and Mediæval Society (1928), p. 21.

5   Oxford, Bodleian, Laud misc. 482, ecclesiastical canons, etc., in Anglo-Saxon, s. xi, with a few glosses in the 'tremulous' Worcester hand. The manuscript was one of those used by John Joscelyn (see above, p. 10).

6   Oxford, Bodleian, Bodley 81 (*S.C.* 2269), the *De lingua*, s. xiii, ascribed commonly, but incorrectly, to Grosseteste. The writing on the parchment label, 'Nonnulli tractatus de diversis materiis', is in one of the Worcester label-writing hands (see above, p. 70).

7   Oxford, Bodleian, Bodley 442 (*S.C.* 2383), Hilarius, *De trinitate*, finely written in the twelfth century. 'Liber *sancte marie Wygorn*' quem exposuit frater *Ricardus* de Bromwico *monachus* eiusdem loci Philippo de Lustushulle pro uno paruo libello distinctionum super psalterium et tabula super originalibus Sancti Augustini' (s. xiv).[2] The words in italics have been erased: a reagent has been used on them and *Wygorn*' and *monachus* are not now legible. The manuscript was deposited as a caution in the Robury chest at Oxford in 1491.

8   Oxford, Bodleian, Rawlinson C. 428, Liber sextus decretalium, etc., s. xiv in. 'Liber sancte marie Wigorn' per fratrem Henricum Fouke monachum eiusdem loci'.[2] The place-name has been erased, but can be read by ultra-violet light. The manuscript was used by Archbishop Parker and by John Joscelyn (see above, p. 10, note 5).

9   London, British Museum, Royal 5 C. vi, Augustinus, *De Musica*, etc., s. xiv (see above, p. 8, note 5).

10   London, British Museum, Royal 11 B. ii, *Quadripartitus*, etc., s. xii–xiii in. (see above, p. 8, note 5).

11, 12, 13   London, British Museum, Harley 1659 and Cotton Otho C. xvi; Oxford, Bodleian, Bodley 113. See above, pp. 9, 11, 13.

[1] For John Musard see *The Journal of Prior William More* (Worc. Hist. Soc. 1914), pp. i–iv.
[2] For Henry Fouke and Richard of Bromwich see Floyer's introduction to the 1906 catalogue, p. xv.

ADDENDUM

NOTE ON BODLEIAN, HATTON 30 (*see above, p. 17*)

The name 'Mr Herle' is found on the first leaf. This is presumably Thomas Hurle, prebendary of Worcester, 1561–86.

London, British Museum, Royal MS. 4 A. ix, Leviticus glo., s. xii, from the Theyer collection. The note 'Willielmus Hanbury perlegit a.d. 1527' on the cover and the name of John Multon (s. xvi) at the end show this to be a Worcester manuscript. Both Hanbury and Multon appear in the list of forty-one monks who acknowledged the Royal Supremacy, 17 Aug., 1534.

INDEX

OF EXTANT MANUSCRIPTS REFERRED TO[1]

[1] Manuscripts now at Worcester and mentioned only in the lists on pp. 4, 7, 29, 31–61, 69–74 are not included in this index. Medieval manuscripts which were not at Worcester in the Middle Ages and post-medieval manuscripts are in italics.

GENERAL INDEX

(Entries relating to the pre-dissolution period are in italics)

Printed in the United States
By Bookmasters